March 2005

בס"ד

Crown Jewels

Sichos in which the Rebbe expanded the Conceptual Frontiers of Chassidic Thought

FROM THE WORKS OF
THE LUBAVITCHER REBBE
RABBI MENACHEM M. SCHNEERSON

Volume I

Translated by
Rabbi Eliyahu Touger

Sichos In English
788 Eastern Parkway
Brooklyn, New York 11213

5759 • 1998

CROWN JEWELS

Published and Copyrighted © by
SICHOS IN ENGLISH
788 EASTERN PARKWAY • BROOKLYN, N.Y. 11213
TEL. (718) 778-5436

ISBN 1-8814-0041-7

5759 • 1998

CREDITS
Rochel Chana Schilder for editing.
Rabbi Aharon Leib Raskin for checking the authenticity of the text
and supplying additional references and source material.
Yosef Yitzchok Turner for designing the layout and typography.
Rabbi Yonah Avtzon for preparing text for publication.
Avrohom Weg for designing the cover.

Table of Contents

Publisher's Foreword

We are all familiar with the Alter Rebbe's parable concerning the crown jewel crushed to make an elixir to heal the king's son.[1] Often, emphasis is placed on the uniqueness of the sacrifice made by the king, who willingly sacrifices his precious jewel for his son's sake.

In the analogue, this means that because of the spiritual descent of the Jewish people, G-d is willing to sacrifice *P'nimiyus HaTorah*, His crown jewel as it were, so that the Jewish people would be able to continue their Divine service.

There is, however, another dimension to the story. While the jewel is in the king's diadem, it is accessible to him alone. When it is crushed and poured into the son's mouth and some — continues the parable — even spills to the floor, it becomes accessible to others and they can assimilate it.

In the analogue, this means that the importance of disseminating *Chassidus* is not merely its therapeutic virtues, that it will enable the Jews to maintain their Divine service despite the challenges of the material nature of the times. Instead, there is a more intrinsic message. Since it is the crown jewel, *Toraso shel Mashiach,* "the teachings of *Mashiach,*"[2] through its dissemination, the spiritual mindset that

---

1. *Igros Kodesh* of the Rebbe Rayatz, Vol. III, p. 326ff.; *Sefer HaSichos 5688,* p. 19.
2. See *On the Essence of Chassidus.*

will characterize the Redemption now becomes accessible to all, enabling everyone to anticipate the Redemption in their hearts, minds, and lives.

Beginning with the Baal Shem Tov, in every generation the crown jewel was ground more thoroughly and spread further. *Chassidus* was transformed from the lofty spiritual heights into a message which could be understood intellectually by wider audiences and internalized within their conduct.

It is not for a chassid to rank the Rebbeim. This said; it is quite obvious that in no previous generation was *Chassidus* ever spread to as wide and as varied a public as it is today. Jews from all backgrounds and ways of life are attracted to the Rebbe and invigorated spiritually by his teachings.

What is most unique about those teachings is the way the Rebbe ground the crown jewel, i.e., how his teachings take the deepest spiritual insights and communicate them in a form which can be appreciated by people at large. On one extreme, even people from the most secular of backgrounds and young children are inspired by his teachings. They were not merely charged emotionally by the Rebbe's charisma. He prompted them to think, exposed them to radical insights into fundamental Jewish ideas, and gave them the conceptual tools required to grasp them.

Simultaneously, intellectual giants and learned scholars would pore over these same texts, amazed at the profundity of the Rebbe's ideas and the simple, unassuming manner in which they are presented. Concepts hinted at in a word or through an inflection in the chassidic texts of previous generations are spelled out in a straight-forward, logical exposition.

This unique combination of opposites will characterize the revelations of the Era of the Redemption. For *Mashiach* will reveal the most profound spiritual truths and make them evident to all mankind, even to simple people and children. Since we are at — indeed in the process of crossing — the threshold of Redemption, the Rebbe's teachings present us with a foretaste of these ideas so that we can assimilate them within our thought processes, spread them to others, and in this manner, bring that future era ever so much closer.

A DIFFERENT MEANS OF EXPOSITION

The medium through which the Rebbe's ideas are presented is also different. In previous generations, the Rebbeim had communicated deep spiritual concepts primarily through *maamarim,* chassidic discourses that require intense concentration and study to comprehend. The Rebbe also delivered *maamarim,* over 1500 of them. Nevertheless, the primary medium through which the Rebbe taught was *sichos,* "talks." These constituted the bulk of the time he spent at *farbrengens,* and the almost forty volumes of *Likkutei Sichos,* "Collected Talks," are the largest single repository of the Rebbe's wisdom which he personally edited and prepared for publication.

Studying a *maamar* forces you to stretch your intellectual powers. The ideas, the manner in which they are presented, and the conceptual flow are different from our ordinary train of thought. You are compelled to adopt a different conceptual approach.

A *sichah* is less challenging. The Rebbe talks to you. Certainly, the ideas may be difficult, but the thrust is directed to the reader. Instead of asking the reader to change his manner of thinking, the Rebbe reaches out to him and presents the concepts in a format that makes their comprehension less formidable. Our efforts can be focused on the ideas themselves instead of struggling to grasp the format in which they are presented.

THE *SICHOS* CHOSEN

We wanted to make these resources available to the English-reading public so that those who did not have access to these ideas in the original would be able to appreciate how the Rebbe expanded the conceptual frontiers of *Chassidus*. A problem arouse, however, for the Rebbe's works are manifold, and we had to make a selection. What would determine which *sichos* we chose?

Every *chassid* treasures certain *sichos* as "crown jewels," talks in which he feels the Rebbe shared his deepest spiritual resources with us. In this series, we chose those *sichos* which we believe most aptly fit that description. Although many other *sichos* could also have been included in this collection, the ones which we did chose, however, all present *chiddushim*, new insights, which clarify fundamental spiritual concepts.

THE MANNER OF PRESENTATION

In contemplating this project, we debated whether to present the *sichos* as adaptations — essays in which the writer digests the Rebbe's ideas and presents them in his own words — or translations in which the thought pattern and the conceptual development used by the Rebbe is preserved and shared.

Each approach has an advantage. An adaptation is user-friendly. It explains more, expanding certain ideas, telescoping others, so that the reader will be able to proceed through the text with less difficulty. A translation, by contrast, will not be as easy to comprehend, but it preserves the intellectual nuances which the Rebbe labored to communicate.

Before going further, let me share a brief story. Approximately a century ago, the chassidic classic, *Likkutei Torah*, was out of print. One of the chassidim, Reb Anshel Aronovitch took it upon himself to prepare the text for reprinting, editing it so carefully that he corrected more than three thousand textual errors.

With what he felt was well-earned pride, he showed his work to another vintage chassid, Reb Dovid Tzvi Chein. When his colleague failed to respond with enthusiasm, Reb

Anshel asked him why his work had not found favor in his eyes.

"Your text will revolutionize the way people study *Likkutei Torah*," his colleague explained. "Up until now, when a chassid would read a passage which did not make sense, he would stop, weigh the matter back and forth in his mind, consider the concept from all vantage points, and if, after this process of give and take, the concept still was confounding, he would conclude that there was a printing error. Now, with your text, the ideas will go down like water, and the reader won't pause to think them over."

The *sichos* which we chose for this series require thought; they are not easy reading. Were they to "go down like water," the profundity of their message might pass some readers by. Therefore, we presented them in full and complete translation, including all the references and footnotes that exist in the Rebbe's original text. Nevertheless, to make the text more accessible to our readers, we included:

a) bracketed additions — explanations set off by square brackets [ ]; parentheses ( ) and squiggle-brackets { } are part of the Rebbe's text;

b) translator's notes in the footnotes.

SPREADING THE WELLSPRINGS

When *Mashiach* told the Baal Shem Tov[3] that he would come when "the wellsprings of your teachings spread outward," he was describing a natural process of causation. As the *Rambam* writes,[4] the fundamental dimension of the Era of the Redemption will not be the Jews' dominion over the gentile powers or the prosperity that will permeate existence, but the revelation of inner, spiritual truth and the

---

3. See the letter from the Baal Shem Tov to his brother-in-law, R. Gershon Kitover, published in *Ben Poras Yosef* and *Kesser Shem Tov*.
4. *Mishneh Torah, Hilchos Melachim* 12:4-5.

dissemination of that truth throughout all existence. "The world will be filled with the knowledge of G-d as the waters cover the ocean bed."[5]

This will not come about as the result of an arbitrary Divine fiat. G-d's desire is that our material world become a dwelling for Him,[6] and for that dwelling be fashioned by man. Hence, it is the dissemination of inner, spiritual truth that will anticipate the Redemption, giving us a foretaste of the insights to be revealed. And in doing so, it will precipitate the coming of that era, for this creates a climate of spiritual awareness throughout the world.

May the study of the Rebbe's teachings hasten the time when "those who repose in the dust will arise and sing,"[7] and we will hear new teachings from the Rebbe. May this take place in the immediate future.

Sichos In English

14th Day of Kislev, 5759
70th Wedding Anniversary of
the Rebbe and the Rebbetzin נ"ע

---

5. *Yeshayahu* 11:9.
6. *Midrash Tanchuma, Parshas Bechukosai*, sec. 3; *Tanya*, ch. 36.
7. Cf. *Isaiah* 26:19.

Lech Lecha

Likkutei Sichos, Vol. V, p. 57ff.

I. As mentioned on frequent occasions, it is doubtful that [any of] the names of the weekly Torah portions are cited in the *Talmud*.[1] [In contrast, all of the names of the books of the *Tanach* are mentioned in that source.[2] And similarly, the *Mishnah*[3] and the *Gemara*[4] refer to the names of almost all

---

1.   *Megillah* 29b does mention the name of readings *VeAtah Tetzaveh* and *Ki Sissa*, and *Megillah* 31a mentions the reading *VeZos HaBerachah*. It can, however, be explained that what is being referred to are the first words of the reading, rather than the name of the reading *per se*.* We do find, however, that *Rashi* (*Sotah* 40b) interprets [the Talmud's words] "and reads *Acharei Mos*" in a manner that indicates that it is the name of the entire passage.**

   *   A parallel to this can be seen in the works of the *Rambam* (*Mishneh Torah, Hilchos Tefillah* 13:1) who refers to the readings *Eleh Toldos* and *VaYomer Adonai el Avram*, although when he refers to the passages by name (in his *Seder Tefillos*), he calls them *Toldos Noach* and *Lech Lecha*.

   **   In contrast, the *Mishnah* (*Megillah* 30b) mentions *Acharei Mos* after speaking of "the passage concerning the festivals," indicating that it is not referring to the passage by name.

   This distinction allows us to understand why in the tractate *Sotah*, *Rashi* states "the intent is only the first passage," although he does not make such a statement in *Megillah* which is a prior tractate. We cannot say that in the tractate *Megillah*, he relies on the statements that he will make later in the tractate of *Sotah* (see *Yad Malachi, Klallei Rashi, Klal* 9 and the sources which he cites). [Rather the explanation is that in *Megillah*, it is unnecessary for *Rashi* to clarify this point, because the *Talmud* is referring only to the first words of the reading. In *Sotah*, by contrast, the *Talmud* is referring to the reading by name. Therefore *Rashi* must clarify that the intent is only the first passage and not the entire reading.]

2.   *Bava Basra* 14b.

3.   See the conclusion of the tractate of *Keilim* which mentions the tractate's name.

4.   As mentioned in the texts of the later scholars in the order of the tractates.*

   Berachos (*Bava Kamma* 30a, see the *Rashba's* commentary), *Peah* (*Bava Metzia* 10a), *Terumos* (*Pesachim* 34a), *Kilayim* (*Jerusalem Talmud, Kilayim* 6:3),

the tractates of the *Talmud*].[5] Nevertheless, there is sufficient evidence to indicate that the names of the weekly
portions are [rooted in our] Torah [heritage]. [Indeed,] for
over a thousand years,[6] it has been Jewish custom to use
these names to refer to these portions.[7]

A conclusion can certainly be drawn from a comparison
[to the following law]: With regard to [the establishment of

Eruvin (*Eruvin* 79a), *Yoma* (*Yoma* 14b), *Rosh HaShanah* (*Taanis* 2a), *Chagigah*
(*Zohar*, Vol. III, p. 223b), *Taanis* (*op. cit.*, p. 247b), *Yevamos* (*op. cit.*, p. 276a),
Kesubos (*Sotah* 2a), *Nedarim* (*Ibid.*), *Nazir* (*Ibid.*), *Sotah* (*Ibid.*), *Bava Kamma*
(*Bava Kamma* 102a, *Zohar*, Vol. III, p. 198a), *Bava Metzia* (*Ibid.*), *Bava Basra*
(*Ibid.*, as "the third *Bava*"), *Sanhedrin* (*Sanhedrin* 41b), *Makkos* (*Sh'vuos* 2b),
Sh'vuos (*Ibid.*), *Ediyos* (*Berachos* 27a, as *Bechirasa* {note *Rashi's* commentary}),
Avodah Zarah (*Avodah Zarah* 14b), *Avos* (*Bava Kamma* 30a, see the commen-
taries of Rabbeinu Chananel and the *Rashba*), *Semachos*, one of the smaller
tractates (*Kesubos* 28a, as *Evel Rabasi*), *Kallah*, one of the smaller tractates
(*Shabbos* 114a), *Zevachim* (*Bava Metzia* 109b as *Shechitas Kodshim* {See *Rashi's*
commentary}), *Menachos* (*Menachos* 7a), *Bechoros* (*Beitzah* 28a), *Tamid* (*Yoma*
14b), *Middos* (*Ibid.* 16a), *Negayim* (*Chagigah* 14a, see also *Ibid.* 11a; one might,
however, say that reference is to the subject and not to the name of the tractate), *Ohelos* (*Eruvin* 79a), *Nidah* (Jerusalem Talmud, *Berachos* 2:6, *Zohar*, Vol. III,
p. 276a), *Machshirin* (Jerusalem Talmud, *Shabbos* 7:2), *Tvul Yom* (Jerusalem Talmud, *Berachos* 3:4), *Uktzin* (*Berachos* 20a).

---

* [Although there are more references,] we have cited only one reference for the
name of each tractate of the *Talmud*

5. And from these we can draw conclusions with regard to the names of the
other tractates of the *Talmud*. See the *Rambam's* Introduction to his Commentary on the *Mishnah*.

6. Many of the names of the Torah readings are mentioned in R. Saadia Gaon's
Siddur in the section concerning the reading of the Torah. ([Some of the
names used by R. Saadia Gaon differ from those used today,] e.g., he calls
Parshas Tazria, Isha, and *Parshas Metzora, Zos Tihiyeh*.* The names of all the
Torah readings are mentioned in the *Rambam's Mishneh Torah*, [the conclusion
of *Sefer Ahavah*], *Seder Tefillos*.

---

* Based on the above, questions may be asked of those who follow the custom of referring [to *Parshas Metzora*] with the name *Taharah* [in keeping
with the practice of] choosing complimentary wording. For it would be
more proper of them to use the name *Zos Tihiyeh* which is mentioned by R.
Saadia Gaon and the *Rambam* (*loc. cit.*). (See *Likkutei Sichos*, Vol. VII, p.
104, note 40, [where this question is discussed].)

7. See *Rashi's* commentary to the Torah which mentions several of the names of
the Torah readings (*Bereishis* 47:2, *Shmos* 19:11, 25:7, *et al*).

a person's identity so that] his name may be used on a legal document, there is an affirmed decision in Torah law that a name which a person has been known to use for 30 days, is his name.[8] How much more so then, with regard to the names of the Torah portions which have been known to be used for over a thousand years, and have been used by the leaders and teachers of the Jewish people, must we conclude that the association between these names and the weekly Torah portions is [not merely a factor of coincidence, but rather] stems from our Torah heritage.

Accordingly, one may conclude that the name which [our] Torah [heritage] has determined for a particular reading reflects the inner content of the entire reading.[9] We are forced to accept this conclusion even if one will say that the names of the Torah readings were chosen [merely] because these are the first words of that passage.[10] For in practice, (according to the Torah,) these are the names by which the entire Torah reading is called. {And with regard to the Torah, one cannot say that this is simply a matter of coincidence, for even with regard to worldly matters, there is nothing that happens solely by chance.[11]} Thus we must assume that the name of a Torah reading carries within it the inner message of the entire reading.[12]

---

8. *Bava Basra* 167b; *Shulchan Aruch, Choshen Mishpat* 49:3; *Rama, Even HaEzer* 120:3.

9. [Although] there are differences of opinion [with regard to] the names [of certain Torah readings, this does not present a problem]. For even with regard to actual *halachic* practice, there are often differences of opinion [among the Sages], and "These and these are the words of the living G-d" (*Eruvin* 13b).

10. Moreover, this is not [entirely] true. For the names of the Torah readings of *Noach* and *Toldos* (according to our present custom, in contrast to the names used by the *Rambam* in *Seder Tefillos*) [which do not mention the first word of the reading]. See *Likkutei Sichos*, Vol. VII, p. 25, note 40, [where this subject is discussed].

11. See *Rambam, Mishneh Torah, Hilchos Taanios* 1:3. See also *Likkutei Sichos*, Vol. IX, p. 181, and the sources mentioned there. See also sec. VIII of this *sichah*.

12. It can be explained that the name of the Torah reading is taken from its first words, because the beginning [of the reading], its "head," contains within it

This concept can be applied to this week's Torah reading, *Parshas Lech Lecha*. All of the points which are later mentioned in the Torah reading — even the last verse — share the same message — *Lech Lecha* — "Go for yourself."[13]

II. For a Jew (beginning from the first Jew, Avraham, [whose Divine service is described in] our Torah reading), *halichah* (*Lech*) — literally going, [in this context, progress] — indicates advancing towards the fundamental purpose of his creation which is [— in the *Mishnah's* words[14] —] "to serve My Creator," i.e., to progress higher in his Divine service. Certainly, this applies with regard to the directive to be taken from the phrase *Lech Lecha*,[15] which can be interpreted [on the non-literal level of *Derush*] as "Go to yourself,"[16] i.e., Avraham our Patriarch was commanded to proceed to the essence of his being, the very root of his soul. Certainly, progress of this nature points toward a very high ascent.

The above, however, raises a question: This concept appears to characterize the beginning of the Torah reading which relates that Avraham carried out [G-d's] command:[17] "Go for yourself from your land, from your birthplace, and from your father's home" and journeyed to *Eretz Yisrael*. And within *Eretz Yisrael* itself, he was "journeying steadily to the south,"[18] i.e., proceeding in the direction of Jerusalem and the *Beis HaMikdash*.[19] This reflects progress "from

---

the entire reading, [as the head contains the life-force for all the limbs of the body].

13. [*Rashi* in his commentary on the verse explains that "for yourself" means for your own benefit, that the journey will bring Avraham advantages that he could not have accrued otherwise.]
14. The conclusion of tractate *Kiddushin*.
15. For the name of the Torah reading is [not merely *Lech*, but] *Lech Lecha*.
16. See the commentary of R. Moshe Alshich to the Torah, which is cited and explained in the *maamar* entitled *Lech Lecha*, 5702 and 5705, *et al.*
17. *Bereishis* 12:1.
18. *Ibid.*:9
19. *Bereishis Rabbah*, the conclusion of sec. 39, *Rashi's* commentary to the verse.

strength to strength,"²⁰ advancing to higher levels of holiness.

Afterwards, however, the Torah reading relates:²¹ "There was a famine in the land, and Avram descended to Egypt," recounting that Avraham had to leave *Eretz Yisrael* and descend to Egypt. How is it possible that this descent would be in harmony (— and indeed, be alluded to —) by the name *Lech Lecha* — which indicates a continuous advance to higher levels?

III. There is a further point: Not only was Avraham's journey to Egypt a descent, as the Torah states: "And Avram descended," (i.e., a spiritual, [as well as a physical] descent), but the cause which motivated his descent — the famine — brought about an even greater concealment [of G-dliness].

For when Avraham left his birthplace, G-d promised him:²² "I will make you a great nation. I will bless you and expand your renown." And yet, when he came "to the land which I will show you,"²³ a famine set in, and Avraham was forced to leave the land.

It is true that this was a test,²⁴ and through overcoming this challenge (as the *Midrash* relates:²⁵ "He did not become upset or protest"), he was able to reach a higher level.²⁶ Nevertheless, the intent of Avraham's journey was not merely to elevate his own self to a higher level. Instead, [his mission was outer-directed:] To cite an analogy employed

---

20. Cf. *Tehillim* 84:8.
21. *Bereishis* 12:10.
22. *Bereishis* 12:2.
23. *Ibid.*:1.
24. *Bereishis Rabbah* 40:2; *Pirkei d'Rabbi Eliezer*, ch. 26; *Avos DeRebbe Nossan* 32:2; *Rashi's* commentary to this verse; the commentary of *Rashi* and *Rambam* to *Avos* 5:3.
25. *Bereishis Rabbah, loc. cit.*
26. See *Bereishis Rabbah* 55:1; *Ramban,* commentary to *Bereishis* 22:1; *Likkutei Torah, Devarim,* p. 19b ff.; *Derech Mitzvosecha* 185b ff.; *et al.*

by the *Midrash*:[27] There was a vial of perfume kept in a corner and its fragrance had not spread. By taking the vial and carrying it from place to place, its fragrance began to spread. So too, G-d told Avraham, "Journey from place to place, and your renown will increase within the world."

Thus the intent of Avraham's journey was that wherever he would journey, G-d's name would become known and sanctified. This is the true meaning [of G-d's promise that] Avraham's renown would increase.[28] For [Avraham's identity was subsumed to G-d to the extent that] his own renown was identified with G-d's renown.

From this can be understood that when Avraham arrived in *Eretz Yisrael*, and immediately thereafter a famine broke out, G-d's name was not sanctified. On the contrary, the gentile nations had the opportunity to complain that the famine came about because of the arrival of a Jew who served G-d. Thus this element of the narrative appears to run contrary to the entire intent of *Lech Lecha*.

IV. There is an additional factor. Avraham's descent into Egypt caused Sarah to be taken into Pharaoh's home. Although G-d protected [her] and nothing undesirable happened; (indeed, Pharaoh did not even touch her),[29] the very fact that Sarah was taken into Pharaoh's home reflects an awesome descent. (In particular, [this is true] for as is

---

27. *Bereishis Rabbah* 39:2.
28. Otherwise, according to the simple meaning of the verse, the rationale for G-d's promise "I will... expand your renown" is difficult to understand. Avraham [had no self-consciousness whatsoever]; he represented the ultimate of *bittul*, as reflected by the verse (*Bereishis* 18:27): "I am but dust and ashes." Thus the question is raised (*Alshich*; the *maamar* entitled *Lech Lecha*, 5667): "How is it possible that Avraham would desire greatness and prominence?" In resolution, the *maamar* explains that the expanded renown which G-d promised Avraham was the ability to "draw down the level of His essential name." Note the explanation in that source.
29. *Midrash Tanchuma, Lech Lecha*, sec. 8.

well known,[30] [taking Sarah] enabled Pharaoh to receive nurture from the realm of holiness.)

Moreover, we see that Avraham's very approach to Egypt brought about a descent within his own character, as reflected in [the fact that] *at that time*,[31] [he told Sarah],[32] "Now I know that you are an attractive woman."

The Baal Shem Tov explains[33] that statement as follows: Our Sages state:[34] "The Patriarchs are the Divine chariot," [i.e., just as a chariot has no will of its own and is no more than a vehicle to transport the person driving it, so, too, the Patriarchs had no thought of their personal identity; their intent was merely to publicize G-dliness throughout the world]. Since Avraham was "a chariot" for G-d, and "his thoughts were always attached to the [sublime] root of thought," it was not until [his descent to Egypt] that he realized that Sarah was an attractive woman. Certainly, he

---

30. See *Or HaTorah, Lech Lecha.*
31. In contrast, before that time [he did not appreciate her beauty] (*Bava Basra* 16a; *Midrash Tanchuma, loc. cit.; Zohar,* Vol. I, p. 81b; the first (and fundamental) interpretation given in *Rashi's* commentary to the verse). From this, it is obvious that this degree of modesty was a manifestation of the physical qualities of Avraham and Sarah.*

(See note 70 which explains that according to the simple interpretation {which is the intent of *Rashi's commentary**}, the "deeds of the Patriarchs" are manifestations of their physical qualities.)

---

* See *Rashi's* commentary which speaks of "the modesty which they both possessed." Similarly, the *Zohar, loc. cit.,* speaks of "the great modesty shared between them." It is possible that for this reason, *Rashi* mentions that this interpretation is based on "*Midrash Aggadah,*" (instead of saying "Our Sages commented" or the like), because from the *Gemara* itself, it would appear that the modesty was Avraham's [virtue] alone.
** Although *Rashi* states that this interpretation is based on "*Midrash Aggadah,*" everything contained in *Rashi's* commentary to the Torah is related to the simple meaning of the text. (See *Likkutei Sichos,* Vol. V, p. 1, note 2.)

32. *Bereishis* 12:11.
33. As quoted in the *Maor Einayim,* the conclusion of *Parshas Shmos,* entry *Vizehu Rabbos Machshavos.*
34. *Bereishis Rabbah* 47:6, 82:6. [See the explanation of this statement in *Tanya,* ch. 34.]

had seen her previously.[35] Nevertheless, since his thought was always focused "beyond the limits of physical sight," [her appearance did not make an impression upon him]. When, however, he approached Egypt, this made (albeit in a refined manner[36]) an impression upon him, and "he descended from his spiritual rung, [to the point where] thoughts [from the material frame of reference, stemming] from the destruction of the vessels"[37] came to him. And as a result, he first realized that Sarah was an attractive woman.

Thus explanation is certainly necessary. How can all the above matters that are included within this Torah reading be referred to with the name *Lech Lecha* which, as above, connotes an ascent from strength to strength?

V. To clarify the above, we have to explain the inner meaning of our Sages' statement: "The deeds of the Patriarchs are a sign for their descendants." The intent is not merely that the deeds of the Patriarchs serve as an indicator; that what happened to the Patriarchs will happen to their descendants. Instead, the intent is that the deeds of the Patriarchs are a precipitator,[38] setting in motion [the factors] that cause the same pattern to recur for posterity.[39]

---

35. For "It is forbidden for a man to consecrate a woman until he sees her" (*Kiddushin* 41a). This resolves the question raised by the *Maharsha* in his *Chidushei Aggados* to *Bava Basra, loc. cit.*

36. See sec. VI, note 45.

37. [Trans. Note: Reference is being made to the destruction of the vessels of the spiritual realm of *Tohu* whose descent established the mindset of spiritual challenge that prevails within our material world.]

38. We find an even more encompassing explanation given with regard to the signs that determine whether an animal is *kosher* or not — that they bring about, not only inform us of, the animal's status. See the *Tzofnas Pane'ach* to the *Rambam, Mishneh Torah, Hilchos Maachalos Assuros* 1:1. [See also *Likkutei Sichos,* Vol. I, p. 222, where this concept is explained.]

39. This is also reflected in the example of the prophets cited by the *Ramban* in his commentary to *Bereishis* 12:6. See also the conclusion of sec. 40 in *Bereishis Rabbah* which quotes G-d as telling Avraham: "Go out and triumph on the way before your descendants." See also the explanation given in *Likkutei Sichos,* Vol. V, p. 80, with regard to the *mitzvos* performed by the Patriarchs.

In this vein, the *Zohar*[40] explains that Avraham's descent into Egypt led to the exile in Egypt, and the fact that "Avraham ascended from Egypt,"[41] brought about [the Jews'] ultimate exodus from that land. [The causality is of more than a general nature; the particulars also match.] Avraham left Egypt "heavily laden with herds, silver, and gold."[42] And as a result, it was promised that when the Jews would leave Egypt, they "would depart with great wealth."[43]

[Similarly,] the spiritual factor that led to the Exodus also had its roots in our ancestors' conduct. It is explained[44] that the Jews were redeemed from Egypt because the women guarded themselves from immorality. This merit stemmed from Sarah's conduct when, despite the fact that she was taken to Pharaoh's palace, she perverted immoral conduct. This granted her descendants the potential to protect themselves against lewdness. Although they lived in Egypt, a depraved land, the Egyptians were unable to exercise any control over the Jewish women, just as Pharaoh was not able to even touch Sarah.[45]

VI. On this basis, we can explain how the inner intent of Avraham's descent to Egypt is alluded to in *Parshas Lech Lecha*. For the ultimate purpose of Avraham's descent into Egypt was to ascend "heavily laden with herds, silver, and gold,"[46] just as the exile into Egypt was intended so that[47]

---

40. Vol. I, p. 81b.
41. *Bereishis* 13:1.
42. *Ibid.*:2.
43. *Ibid.* 15:14.
44. See *Shir HaShirim Rabbah* 4:12.
45. See *Or HaTorah, Lech Lecha* and see *Tzror HaMor,* commenting on *Bereishis* 12:10.
46. Similar concepts can be explained with regard to "the Egyptian-like thoughts that came to [Avraham]." They were intended "so that he could elevate them to their source... and not to disturb him.... This was considered as a greater dimension of slavery for him" (*Maor Einayim, loc. cit.*).

    Nevertheless, on a revealed level, this was a descent from [Avraham's] level. Thus [by acknowledging Sarah's beauty], he was saying [as it were]: "Now I know that I have fallen from my level." It was only through the spiri-

"they would depart with great wealth," having elevated the sparks of holiness of that land. Thus the descent was the first phase of the ascent.

To site a parallel: The analysis of a subject in the *Babylonian Talmud*[48] begins with questions and dialectic inquiry which on the surface veil and conceal the Torah's insights[49] (in contrast to the *Jerusalem Talmud* which follows the pattern of direct light[50]). Nevertheless, the didactic process and the many questions raised enable us to penetrate to the depths of the *halachah* to a far greater extent than is possible through the study of the *Jerusalem Talmud*. For this reason, whenever there is a difference of opinion between the *Babylonian Talmud* and the *Jerusalem Talmud*, the *halachah* follows the *Babylonian Talmud*.[51]

With regard to the veiling and concealment that exists within the *Babylonian Talmud*, it is obvious that the study of the questions is part of the clarification of Torah law that comes about as a result. Similarly, with regard to Avraham's descent into Egypt, since this descent was a necessary preparatory step to his ascent "heavily laden with herds...," it also must be seen as one of the phases of that ascent.

---

tual service implied by "Please say that you are my sister" that "the[se] thoughts... came to him... to elevate them to their source."

47. See *Likkutei Sichos*, Vol. III, p. 828ff. See also the passage from *Maor Einayim* cited previously.

48. {[There is an intrinsic connection between these concepts and the content of this *sichah*,] because the approach of the *Babylonian Talmud*} came about as a result of exile. And as explained previously, the reasons and the source for all the exiles is the Egyptian exile (see the sources referred to in note 52). That exile in turn came as a result of Avraham's descent to Egypt as explained in sec. V.

49. For, as stated in the *Zohar*, Vol. III, *Raya Mehemna*, *Parshas Nasso*, p. 124b, and explained in *Tanya*, *Iggeres HaKodesh*, Epistle 26, "A question stems from the side of evil."

50. *Shaarei Orah*, the *maamar* entitled *B'Chof Hei B'Kislev*, ch. 54ff. *Sefer HaMaamarim 5708*, p. 121. [I.e., the *Jerusalem Talmud* does not raise questions and contradictions, but instead, explains the laws and concepts in a straightforward manner.]

51. See *Yad Malachi*, the beginning of sec. II.

This concept also applies to our people's later descent into Egypt. Since the purpose and goal of the descent into Egypt is the ultimate ascent and exodus, the descent can be seen as a preparatory phase leading to that ascent.

Similar principles apply with regard to the present exile (for the Egyptian exile is the source for all the subsequent exiles[52]). The intent of this exile is [to elevate the Jews and the world to a higher level], as indicated by our Sages' statement:[53] "The Holy One, blessed be He, did not exile Israel among the nations except for the purpose of having converts gathered to them." ["Converts" here must be understood in an expanded sense, as referring to] the refinement of the sparks of holiness which exist within the exile. Through [this mission], the Jews are elevated to a spiritual level higher than that which existed at the time of the *Beis HaMikdash*, as indicated by the verse:[54] "The glory of this later house will surpass that of the first." Thus it is obvious that this descent is a part of the ascent which is drawing near.

VII. This [produces] a directive for us in our own Divine service. When a person considers the spiritual situation of the world at large, [he may be overwhelmed] by the day-to-day increase of spiritual darkness. As our Sages commented:[55] "The [negative elements][56] of each day are

---

52. See *Likkutei Sichos*, Vol. IX, p.178, note 28.
53. *Pesachim* 87b; *Torah Or*, p. 6a; *Or HaTorah, Lech Lecha*, p. 86a.
54. *Chaggai* 2:19. See *Zohar*, Vol. I, p. 28a, and other sources which explain that the verse refers to the Third *Beis HaMikdash* which will be built by the Holy One, blessed be He.

   Needless to say, this does not represent a contradiction to our Sages' interpretation (*Bava Basra* 3a) that the verse refers to the Second *Beis HaMikdash*. Note *Zohar*, Vol. III, 103a; *Rashba*, Vol. IV, *Responsum* 187, *et al.* (See also *Likkutei Sichos*, Vol. IX, pp. 28-29, note 29.)
55. *Sotah* 49a.
56. [Trans. Note: The actual Hebrew word used is *kilkalaso*, meaning "curse." In the original text, to refrain from using an unfavorable term, the Rebbe did not include it.]

greater than those of the preceding day." This can lead to despair, causing a person to think: "How is it possible for me to muster the strength to endure the darkness and illuminate the world with the light of the Torah and its *mitzvos?*"

In reply, he should understand that all of the descents, veils and concealments are merely external factors. When looking at the inner dynamic, one appreciates that, on the contrary, the world does not control its own destiny. It is being directed by G-d, and we can be certain that G-d's intent is that everything that occurs in the world — even those elements which appear to be darkness and descent — is intended to lead to the world's refinement and elevation. Thus this descent is really merely a preparatory step for — and itself a part of — that ultimate ascent. And thus from day to day, the world is reaching a higher level and becoming more refined, until eventually, it will reach its consummate fulfillment, when it will be realized that it is G-d's dwelling.

VIII. There is, however, still a need for further clarification: It is true that "Man's footsteps are established by G-d,"[57] and that wherever a person goes — even though it appears that he is acting independently, because of his own desires — he is acting because of G-d's desires. (And indeed, [G-d's desire is the source] of his own desire. For these dimensions of man's power of will are sensitive to G-d's will.[58])

This applies with regard to the ordinary, mundane aspects of a person's conduct. The observance of the Torah and its *mitzvos,* by contrast, has been given over to a man's free choice. He can do whatever he wants.[59] He can even perform a sin which is the opposite of G-d's will.

---

57. *Tehillim* 37:23; see the statement of the Baal Shem Tov quoted in the *Mafteichos ViHaaros* to *Likkutei Torah,* p. 18d, *HaYom Yom,* p. 69.

58. See the *maamar* entitled *VaYachalom,* 5708, sec. 10.

59. See the *Rambam, Mishneh Torah, Hilchos Teshuvah,* ch. 5.

[These concepts also relate to our Torah reading. For] the *Ramban*[60] interprets Avraham's descent to Egypt as "a sin which he committed." How can we explain that such an act is, from an inner perspective, an ascent? [By definition, a transgression is the opposite of G-d's will.]

With regard to the exile of the Jewish people as a whole, an explanation can be offered: Although "because of our sins, we were exiled from our land,"[61] the exile itself was brought about by G-d. (It is merely that the reason G-d brought about the exile was our sins.) And since everything which stems from G-d is certainly intended to bring the world to its ultimate purpose, it can be explained that the exile [is not merely a punishment]. Instead, the exile is structured in such a manner that (not only will it remove the blemish and the descent caused by sin,[62] but) it will bring the Jews to a higher level than they experienced at the time of the *Beis HaMikdash*. Hence, [exile] itself is part of the process of ascent.

With regard to Avraham's descent into Egypt, however, the descent itself — at least according to the *Ramban's* interpretation — was against G-d's will. How then is it possible to consider it part of a process of ascent?

IX. On a previous occasion, it was explained at length that the "sins" which the Torah mentions with regard to righteous men and in particular with regard to the Patriarchs cannot be understood as sins in the ordinary conception of the term. For perfect *tzaddikim* do not have an evil inclina-

---

60. In his commentary to *Bereishis* 12:10. See also the *Zohar* on this Torah reading (p. 81b) which states that Avraham went to Egypt "without permission." (Note, however, *Rashi's* commentary to the above verse which states that it was "the Holy One, blessed be He... who induced him to leave [the land].")
61. *Mussaf* liturgy for festivals, *Siddur Tehillat HaShem*, p. 258.
62. This is the purpose of all punishment [and retribution], to wash away the sin (*hagahah, Tanya*, ch. 24).

tion.[63] And with regard to the Patriarchs, since as above, they served as "a chariot" for G-d's will throughout their entire lifetime,[64] evil — the source of all sin — had no place entirely in their makeup.

Instead, for them, sin (חטא), can be understood in an extended context.[65] [When Bat Sheva asked King David to keep his pledge to grant the kingship to her son Shlomo, she told him that otherwise, "I and my son Shlomo will be lacking (חטאים)."[66]] Similarly, with regard to the righteous, חטא, sin, refers to a lack, a deficiency in Divine light; less Divine light is drawn down. To cite a parallel: In the spiritual realms, there is a continuous downward progression of light. On every level, there is less light than on the level that is above it.[67] [Similarly, the Patriarch's "sins" involved reducing the quantity of Divine light; all their actions, however, remained] in the realm of holiness.

The above explanations do not represent a contradiction to the teaching [shared by the Maggid of Mezeritch][68] on

---

63. *Tanya*, chs. 1 and 10. This is particularly true with regard to Avraham our Patriarch, of whom it is said: "He transformed his *yetzer hora* into goodness," which is a higher level than "My heart is a void within me" (*Tehillim* 109:22) which the *Tanya* uses [to describe the level of a complete *tzaddik*]. (See the *Jerusalem Talmud, Berachos* 9:5.)

64. *Tanya*, ch. 23 (p. 28b).

65. *Likkutei Torah, Bamidbar* 82a; the *maamar* entitled *Al Kein Yomru HaMoshlim*, 5691, *et al.*

66. *I Melachim* 1:21.

67. A similar [pattern] can be seen with regard to all the *tzimtzumim* and descents of Divine light in the spiritual realms including the initial *tzimtzum*. All of these are intended for the sake of revelation. Similarly, the "sins" of the Patriarchs [were intended to bring about an increase in holiness], as reflected in the statements of the *Maor Einayim* cited in note 45.

    Nevertheless, as stated in the conclusion of this section, on an external level, this appears as a sin. This can be understood in terms of the explanation given in the *maamar* entitled *Al Kein Yomru HaMoshlim* cited above, that the lack of Divine light caused by the first *tzimtzum* makes it possible for actual sins to be committed.

68. *Kovetz Michtavim LiTehillim*, p. 197. [This source relates that the Maggid told the Alter Rebbe that in *Gan Eden*, he heard the following teaching being taught to schoolchildren by Moshe *Rabbeinu*.]

the verse:[69] "And Avraham fell on his face and laughed and he said within his heart: 'Will [a man who is] 100 years old father a child? Will Sarah who is 90 years old give birth?" [The Maggid explained:]

> The meaning of the verse does not depart from its literal interpretation.[70] If you will ask: How is it possible that Avraham could have doubts[71] with regard to G-d's promise? Know that this stems from the body.[72] For even a holy body is flesh.

[That teaching cannot be interpreted to mean that the Patriarchs were capable of committing sins in a simple sense.] For the teaching itself speaks about "a *holy* body." Hence, sin in a simple sense is not relevant, for in the realm of holiness, there is no conception of evil. Accordingly, the above teaching should be interpreted to mean that the Patriarchs performed these activities because of their bodies. And since their bodies were flesh, these actions were performed in a manner which (from a simple and superficial perspective) could be understood as a sin.[73]

---

69. *Bereishis* 17:17.
70. *Shabbos* 63a.
71. *Rashi*, in his commentary to the verse, explains that Avraham believed G-d's promise (only Sarah did not). Nevertheless, [this should not be understood to mean that the Maggid's explanation departs from the simple interpretation of the verse]. (Indeed, the Maggid states that his explanation was given to schoolchildren.) For there are many different interpretations even within the context of the simple meaning of the Torah. ([In this context,] see the statements of *Rashi* quoted by the *Rashbam* in the beginning of his commentary to *Parshas Vayeishev*.)
72. See *Sichos Parshas Lech Lecha*, 5725 (*Likkutei Sichos*, Vol. V, p. 298ff.), which clarifies that the explanations of [the statement] "the deeds of the Patriarchs" that follow the *Peshat* reflect the manner in which those deeds affect the body, and the explanations which follow the approach of *Derush* relate to the soul. (See *Tanya, Iggeres HaKodesh*, Epistle 23 {p. 137a} which identifies the *Aggadah*, [the aspect of the Torah which follows the approach of *Derush*,] with *P'nimiyus HaTorah*. *P'nimiyus HaTorah* itself is described as "the soul of the Torah.")
73. [The concepts explained above can be understood in terms of] the well-known concept that G-d's name *Elokim* {the source for the *keilim* which parallel the human body (*Tanya, Shaar HaYichud VehaEmunah*, ch. 6, p. 81a)}, though itself one of His holy names, allows for the possibility of nurture to

X. On this basis, we can understand the reason why Avraham's descent to Egypt can be considered as part of his
eventual ascent. For from an inner standpoint, Avraham
acted according to G-d's will.

This explanation is, however, insufficient, for all the
concepts related in the Torah are lessons for every Jew
(even a person who has the potential to commit a sin in a
literal sense). Accordingly, the fact that the Torah tells us
about Avraham's descent to Egypt — which can be interpreted as a sin in a literal sense — in the Torah reading of
Lech Lecha serves as a lesson for every Jew: When he
commits a sin in a literal sense, the sin is against G-d's will.
Nevertheless, he must realize that from an inner standpoint, (even at the time of the sin,) he is in the midst of a
process of continuous ascent.

XI. To explain the above (at least in a concentrated
manner): One of the fundamental principles of faith (even
according to the legal tradition of *Nigleh*[74]) is that G-d is the
only Master within the entire world. Aside from Him, no
other entity has any dominion [or any independent author-
ity]. For all the stars and the spheres[75] — and even the

---

the external forces [i.e., the forces of evil]. {This parallels the explanation
given with regard to the first *tzimtzum* ([which is also referred to as] the
source for the *keilim*) in note 65.}

Similar concepts apply with regard to the revealed Torah, [the body of
Torah law]. (See the previous note [which equates *P'nimiyus HaTorah* with the
soul of the Torah. Thus the revealed Torah parallels "the body."]) Although
the revealed Torah is "G-d's wisdom, without any compound of evil, Heaven
forbid" (*Tanya, Iggeres HaKodesh*, Epistle 26, p. 143b), it allows the possibility
of nurture [for the forces of evil] (see *Kuntres Etz HaChayim*, ch. 12ff.). To cite
a parallel: Noticing the use of the plural in the verse (*Bereishis* 1:26): "Let us
make man," our Sages comment (*Bereishis Rabbah* 8:8): "Let one who desires
to err, err." (Note *Rashi's* commentary to that verse.)

74. See *Mitzvas Achdus HaShem* in *Derech Mitzvosecho* (p. 60b). The explanations to
follow in the text above reflects "the explanation according to *Nigleh*" given
there.

75. [Powers to which astrologers would attribute control over fate.]

angels — are merely "an ax in the hand of the chopper,"[76] functioning only "according to the will and command of G-d."[77] Believing that there are certain entities that have the ability to function according to their independent will runs contrary to the faith in the oneness of G-d. (This applies even if one acknowledges that any activity performed by these entities is performed with power vested in them by G-d, but maintains that these entities have the choice whether to exercise this power or not.)[78]

This also applies with regard to every individual person. Everything that he does, even those matters which affect the Torah and its *mitzvos* (which with regard to them, he has been granted free choice) are dependent on G-d's providence[79] and His will.[80]

---

76. Cf. *Yeshayahu* 10:15.

77. This is the wording used by the *Tzemach Tzedek* in the above source. (See also p. 6a ff.) See also the fifth of the *Rambam's* "Thirteen Principles of Faith" (in his Commentary to the *Mishnah, Sanhedrin* 10:1) which states that neither the constellations or any other heavenly [or earthly] body has free choice.

78. See the sources cited previously.

79. Were this not to be so, there would be no resolution to the question raised by the *Rambam* (*Mishneh Torah, Hilchos Teshuvah* 5:4): "How is it possible for man to do whatever he desires and be granted the potential to control his deeds? Is it possible [for man] to do anything in this world without the will of his Creator?"

The *Rambam* offers the following resolution: "Just as the Creator desired that fire and wind ascend upward... and desired that the other creations follow the nature with which they were endowed, so, too, He desired that man be given license, and for all of his deeds to be under his control.

This resolution, however, appears insufficient, [because the concept that man can have utter free will — even if granted to him by G-d — appears to be a denial of G-d's absolute sovereignty.] For the idolaters who worship the stars because they believe that they have free choice and do not consider them as "an ax in the hand of the chopper" (*Derech Mitzvosecha*, p. 6a), still do not think that their free choice is their independent franchise. Instead, they believe that it is G-d who desired that they have free choice. (See the *Rambam, Mishneh Torah, Hilchos Avodah Zarah* 1:1 who writes: "They believe that this emptiness is His will.") Nevertheless, since the idolaters maintain (according to their [mistaken] conception) that the stars have the authority to do as they desire, this is (not merely an error and foolishness, but also) a denial of His oneness.

There is, however, a fundamental difference [between the Divine providence that governs material concerns and the Divine providence that governs our observance]. With regard to the Divine will that relates to the external dimensions of the world, since it is (the external [dimensions of His] will), it therefore[81] relates to the created beings in a [direct and] immediate manner which is felt within the created beings. As a consequence, it compels the created beings to carry out His will.[82]

G-d's desire that relates to the Torah and its *mitzvos*, by contrast, is (the inner [dimensions of His] will. Thus as a consequence,[83] it is) above the [framework of] creation.[84]

[Thus although the resolution mentioned by the *Rambam* cited above is based on the fact that man's free choice was granted to him by G-d, this also applies, according to the idolaters' mistaken conception, to the free choice of the stars. Hence, according to the *Rambam,* the question can be raised:] What is the difference between the free will of man and the [supposed] free will of the stars?

Therefore it is apparent that we must rely on the explanation to follow in the text above. See also *Likkutei Sichos,* Vol. III, *Parshas Shemini,* note 19.

80. This is the wording used by the Previous Rebbe in the *maamar* entitled *VaYachalom,* 5708, sec. 9. The continuation of the text [in that *maamar*]: "This is the concept of choice with regard to the Torah and its *mitzvos*," indicates that [such observance] is also "dependent on [His] providence."

81. See the *maamar* entitled *ViHu KiChasan,* 5657, sec. V, and the *maamar* entitled *ViEleh Toldos,* 5666.

82. [Trans. Note: The intent appears to be that our world comes into being because G-d desired "a dwelling in the lower worlds," i.e., His will is that the Jews observe the Torah within this material frame of reference. That material framework is thus not desired in its own right; it is needed merely as the setting for the Jews' observance. Accordingly, it is structured according to the dictates of G-d's wisdom, and once it is structured, it is defined. A set pattern is brought into existence that determines the functioning of every being — and every future event — that exists within that framework. Moreover, this "natural order" even restricts G-d Himself as it were. For although He can disrupt the natural order and bring about change within it, this is not His will. For as stated above, His desire is for a dwelling within the lower worlds, that He be recognized within the natural order. Hence, He desires to maintain that natural order without change.]

83. In addition, the external dimension of G-d's will is itself "forced upon Him," (as it were, because of [His desire for] the Torah and its *mitzvos*; [i.e., since G-d desires that the Jews observe the Torah and its *mitzvos*, He is, as it were, compelled to create a framework, the creation at large, where the Torah and

Hence it is not felt within a human being, and does not compel [his conduct].[85] And so, every act of a person[86] that relates to the Torah and its *mitzvos* is performed through his free choice.[87]

XII. Based on the above, it is clear that even the descents that the world at large and every individual person experience and that come as a result of man's deeds performed according to his own free will, are still dependent on G-d's providence. Accordingly, [it is also evident] that they lead to a [positive] purpose. Hence even these descents can be seen as phases in [the accomplishment of] this purpose.

---

its *mitzvos* will be observed]. See the *maamarim* cited in note 79.) Because this desire [compels G-d as it were], it also compels the created beings.

[G-d's] desire for the Torah and its *mitzvos*, in contrast, is not defined or forced upon Him. On the contrary, [as the *Midrash*] (*Bereishis Rabbah* 44:1) states: "What difference does it make [for the Holy One, blessed be He, if one slaughters from the neck or from the back]? and (*ibid.*: 2:5) quotes G-d as saying: "I don't know which I desire, the deeds of [the righteous] or the deeds of [the wicked]." [His desire for the deeds of the righteous is thus only a function of His choice.] Since His desire [for the Torah and its *mitzvos*] is not forced, as it were, it does not compel a person's choice. See also note 86.

84. [Trans. Note: The intent appears to be that G-d's will is undefined and unlimited as He Himself is. Therefore just as within His essence there is the possibility for opposites to exist, opposites — i.e., His desire for the Torah and its *mitzvos* and His willingness to consent to their violation so that a Jew can experience *teshuvah* — also exist within His will.]

85. See ch. 9 of the *maamar* entitled *VaYachalom* which states that the person: "thinks he is acting as a result of his independent will." It is, nevertheless, clearly understood that [man's] free choice in [observing] the Torah and its *mitzvos* {which is "a fundamental principle of great importance, a pillar of the Torah and its commandment[s]" (*Rambam, Hilchos Teshuvah* 5:3)} is genuine; (it is not that man merely thinks that he is choosing his future). Hence, we are forced to say that the meaning of the passage from the *maamar* entitled *VaYachalom* is as explained in the text above. This concept is explicitly stated in the sources mentioned in note 87.

86. Note the expression used by the *Rambam* (*loc. cit.*:1): "This is implied by the Torah's statement (*Bereishis* 3:22): 'Thus man has become like one of Us...,'" i.e., that he has free choice. See also *Likkutei Torah, Vayikra* 38b.

87. See a similar explanation which is given in the *Biurei Zohar* of the *Tzemach Tzedek*, Vol. I, pp. 265-266, and in the *maamar* entitled *Vehayah Ki Savo*, 5672.

Unquestionably, the actual performance of a sin is against G-d's will.[88] Nevertheless, the descent — in the world and within the person — which comes as a consequence of the sin is not contrary to G-d's will.[89] And thus it is not a true descent, but rather a phase in the ascent which comes about through it.

XIII. [Based on the above, we can appreciate] the directive that results from the fact that Avraham's descent into Egypt is related in *Parshas Lech Lecha*: Regardless of the nature of the situation in which a Jew is found, even if he is in a very lowly and degrading situation, and even if he himself was

---

88. Although [committing a sin is against G-d's will, the fact that man can do so] does not minimize G-d's authority or His unity, because [of the uniqueness of G-d's] desire for the Torah and its *mitzvos*. Since this desire is not defined or forced upon Him, Heaven forbid, (as stated in note 83), the sin is of no consequence, nor does it generate concealment for Him (as explained in *Likkutei Sichos*, Vol. VII, p. 23).

[I.e., were G-d's desire for the Torah and its *mitzvos* to be a straightforward cut and dry matter, the fact that a person committed a sin would represent not only a difficulty with regard to that person's relationship with G-d, but a challenge to His sovereignty. For sin is a defiance of His will. And it would represent a contradiction to His absolute unity, for the act of sin could not be at one with Him. Explaining that His desire for the Torah and its *mitzvos* is undefined — He "does not know which [He] desires" — clarifies why a transgression of the Torah and its *mitzvos* does not dispute His authority or His oneness. For even if a person commits a sin, he has not violated G-d's will as it exists in an ultimate sense.]

Although from the standpoint of G-d's choice, He does not desire the deeds of the wicked [and therefore at this level, the questions sin raises with regard to His sovereignty and His oneness would appear legitimate, this also does not represent a theoretical problem]. For His choice stems from His essence which exists in a manner beyond the framework of existence as we know it. [That level] is utterly undefined; no description — either positive or negative — is appropriate for it. Therefore the fact that one acts contrary to this level of G-d's will does not represent a change [in His will, and His will can also include an act that appears, at the outset, to run contrary to His desire]. See also note 93.

89. [To cite a parallel, *Tanya*,] *Iggeres HaKodesh*, Epistle 25 (p. 138b), [explains that] although a person who injures a colleague is given free choice [and is not obligated to harm his fellow man], it was already decreed from Above that the injured party would suffer this harm.

the one who brought himself to this abject state through his choice of evil, [he should have a positive perspective].

[Certainly,] because "he caused himself a loss," "it is appropriate for him to cry and lament his sins and the evil which he brought upon his soul."[90] And yet, the person should not despair and think that all hope is lost for him. For since the situation to which he brought himself came about not only because of his own choice, but because of G-d's providence, it will ultimately lead him (— through *teshuvah* —) to an extremely elevated rung.[91] Through *teshuvah*, he will be able to elevate even the sparks of holiness that are found within his willful transgressions and transform them into merits.[92]

The sins themselves cannot be elevated; on the contrary, "their destruction[93] is their rectification."[94] With regard to

---

90. *Rambam, Mishneh Torah, Hilchos Teshuvah* 5:2.
91. [The uniqueness of the spiritual level attained through *teshuvah*] can be explained in two ways:

   a) Through *teshuvah*, the person can elevate even the sparks of G-dliness within the sins which he purposefully committed, as explained in the text above;

   b) He destroys the sinful acts through his *regret* and *bitterness* over them.

   The second quality (destroying the act of sin) reaches a higher level than the refinement of the sparks of G-dliness. [For to free oneself from the framework of evil and destroy its hold, one must tap the essence of the soul, a spiritual level above any of the sparks of G-dliness that may be elevated. (See *Likkutei Sichos*, Vol. VI, p. 22ff. [translated in this series].)]

   (This concept can be appreciated from the explanation in *Toras Chayim, Shmos*, pp. 332b, 337a. This is also reflected by the fact that *Pirkei Avos* 5:1 and *Tanya*, ch. 22 (p. 27b) mention "to punish the wicked," before "to grant a generous reward to the righteous who subjugate the *sitra achra*." (See also *Likkutei Sichos*, Vol. V, p. 249, note 59.)
92. See *Yoma* 86b.
93. [The sins themselves must be rejected entirely; there is no way that they themselves — in contrast to the G-dly spark they contain — can be elevated.] Although there is nothing apart from G-d, as it is written (*Devarim* 4:35): "There is nothing else aside from Him," nevertheless, we cannot say (that *kelipah* and more particularly,) sins will be able to be elevated and made vessels for G-dliness, for they are the opposite of His will. With regard to them, the concept that "There is nothing else aside from Him," is revealed by the fact that they are of no consequence and need not be reckoned with (as stated in note 88). Therefore "their destruction is their rectification."

the person's own situation, however, he must realize that through the sin, he has been granted the opportunity (in an inner manner which is not openly revealed) to achieve an ascent. For he has the potential [to do *teshuvah*] — and [since] he has been assured that "no one will ever remain estranged from Him,"[95] he will certainly make that potential actual. In doing so, he [will] elevate the sparks of holiness found within these purposeful sins, transforming them into merits which surpass the merits of the *tzaddikim*.

(Adapted from *Sichos Shabbos Parshas Chayei Sarah*, 5713, 5725, *Chag HaShavuos* 5721)

{I.e., in contrast to entities within the realm of holiness, which [reveal G-dliness in a positive manner,] by being united with Him, [entities within the realm of *kelipah* and sins can] never become mediums [for the revelation of G-dliness]. [They reveal G-d's power by being nullified and showing that their existence — i.e., an existence apart from G-d — is of no genuine importance.]}

{G-d's lack of desire for "the deeds of the wicked" is reflected in the fact that "the deeds of the wicked" exist, and yet are nullified. See *Toras Chayim, Shmos*, p. 331b which explains that the forces that oppose holiness are brought into being "to [bring into expression] His attribute of victory." See also the explanation of the phrase "to punish the wicked" in *Tanya*, ch. 22 (p. 27b). See also note 89 above.}

94. Cf. *Keilim* 2:1. See the *maamar* entitled *Noach*, 5670. See also *Likkutei Sichos*, Vol. VII, pp. 22-23, notes 20 and 28.

95. See *II Shmuel* 14:14. [The interpretation of this phrase in the above context has its source in] the Alter Rebbe's ruling, *Hilchos Talmud Torah* 4:3, and *Tanya*, ch. 39, which states: "He will certainly turn in *teshuvah*, for 'no one will ever remain estranged from Him.'"

(The *Rambam* in *Hilchos Teshuvah* 7:5 uses a different [prooftext for a similar concept, because the *Rambam*] is speaking about the Jewish people as a whole, [while the Alter Rebbe is concerned with each individual Jew].)

Vayishlach /
Yud-Tes Kislev

Likkutei Sichos, Vol. XV, p. 281ff.

I. Several interpretations are offered for the verse:[1] "And Yaakov remained alone." Among them:

    a) The *Talmud* states[2] (and this interpretation is quoted — with slightly different wording — by *Rashi* in his commentary to the Torah): "He remained because of small utensils." This is alluded to in [the wording of the verse as well]. As the *Baalei HaTosafos* state:[3] "Do not read לבדו, "alone," but rather לכדו, "for his jug."[4]

    b) The *Midrash* states:[5] "Just as with regard to the Holy One, blessed be He, it is said:[6] "And He is exalted alone;" so, too, with regard to Yaakov, "Yaakov remained alone."

As explained on several occasions,[7] all of the interpretations of a verse (— and certainly of a word —) share an intrinsic connection. When applying this concept to the verse at hand, we must understand: What is the connection

---

1.   *Bereishis* 32:25.
2.   *Chulin* 91a.
3.   This interpretation is also mentioned by Rabbeinu Bachaye (in the name of "our Rabbis") and Rabbi Ovadiah of Bartenura in their commentary to this verse.
4.   See also the *Baal HaTurim* who interprets the term as referring to בית הבד, "an olive press," and *Hadar Zekeinim* [who offer another interpretation, stating: "We know the implication of לבדו...." See also the commentaries to *Rashi*.
5.   *Bereishis Rabbah* 77:1.
6.   *Yeshayahu* 2:17.
7.   See *Likkutei Sichos*, Vol. III, p. 782, *et al.*

between the two interpretations? On the contrary, they appear to have opposite imports.

According to the interpretation offered by the *Talmud*, Yaakov's remaining alone is associated with "small [utensils]," objects that have little importance.[8] {And the word לכדו is interpreted as meaning "for his jug."}

In contrast, according to the *Midrash*, Yaakov's remaining alone reflects a peak of elevation, a state of aloneness[9] which is compared to that of G-d Himself, i.e., His singular oneness. [Moreover, it indicates that such oneness] will be revealed [in a consummate manner] as will take place in the Era of the Redemption, as reflected in the continuation of the prooftext which speaks of "on that day."

II. As is well known, the *Shaloh* writes[10] that the weekly Torah readings contain allusions to all the festivals that fall during the weeks they are read. From this we can conclude that since in many years — as this year — the festival[11] of *Yud-Tes* Kislev falls in the week — or on the *Shabbos* — in which *Parshas Vayishlach*[12] is read, the intent of *Yud-Tes* Kislev is alluded to in that Torah reading.[13]

---

8. This is particularly true in light of the interpretation of the *Kli Yakar* [who explains that Yaakov's preoccupation with his possessions was an expression of spiritual blindness]. See also the interpretation of the Maggid of Mezeritch (*Or Torah*, p. 111a) who explains that Yaakov's forgetting small utensils refers to his loss of minor intellectual faculties.

9. See also *Toras Levi Yitzchak* (p. 11) who associates "And Yaakov remained alone" with the blessing (*Bamidbar* 23:9): "Behold! It is a nation which will dwell in solitude."

10. In the portion of his text entitled *Torah Shebichsav*, the beginning of *Parshas Vayeishev*.

11. This was the wording used by the Alter Rebbe, as quoted in *Likkutei Dibburim*, Vol. I, p. 19b. Note also the expression used by my revered father-in-law, the Rebbe (as quoted in the letter printed as an introduction to *HaYom Yom* and to the pamphlet of *Yud-Tes* Kislev) who would refer to it as "the festival of festivals." (Note the explanation of that term in *Likkutei Sichos*, Vol. V, p. 436ff.

12. Even when *Yud-Tes* Kislev falls in the week of *Parshas Vayeishev*, it is blessed from the preceding *Shabbos*, the *Shabbos* of *Parshas Vayishlach*.

13. See also *Sefer HaSichos 5704*, p. 50 (as mentioned in note 77 at the conclusion of this *sichah*); *Likkutei Sichos*, Vol. I, p. 70, *et al.*

[The connection between the two] can be understood through the preface [of a concept of greater scope].

There are two explanations given for the fact that *Chassidus* was revealed in these later generations (as opposed to the previous generations, [when our people were on a higher spiritual level, to borrow our Sages' expression]:[14] "If those of the early generation were angels, [then we can be considered humans]"):

    a) Because of the manifold spiritual darkness that has continued to swell in the later generations (and in particular, in the era of *ikvesa deMeshicha*, the time when *Mashiach's* approaching footsteps can be heard), it is necessary to tap a higher light which will enable us to overcome that darkness.[15]

    b) To borrow an explanation from the writings of the *AriZal*[16] (which is quoted as *halachah* by the *Magen Avraham*[17] and the *Shulchan Aruch* of the Alter Rebbe[18] — for whom [*Yud-Tes* Kislev] is a day of happiness and redemption): On Friday, one must taste the foods that are prepared for *Shabbos*, (as alluded to in the phrase: "Those who taste of it

---

14. *Shabbos* 112b. [That source states בני מלאכים, lit. "the sons of the angels."] A similar expression is found in the *Jerusalem Talmud, Demai* 1:3. In *Shekalim* 5:1 and in *Bereishis Rabbah* 60:8, the word בני is not used. This is also the version of the text cited by Rav Nissim Gaon in *Shabbos, loc. cit.* and *Tosafos, Shabbos* 12b, entry *Rabbi Nasan*. Both versions are cited by *Dikdukei Sofrim, Shabbos* 112b. See also *Tosafos, Chullin* 5b, entry *Tzaddikim*, which quotes the version "like angels." This is the version quoted in many texts.

15. See *Kuntres Etz HaChayim*, ch. 13, and the letter from the Rebbe Rashab printed on page 82 as an appendix to that text.

    Note also the analogy of the Alter Rebbe [quoted in *HaTamim*, Vol. II, p. 49 (72)] with regard to the son of a king who became sick, and the explanation that the Baal Shem Tov awakened the Jewish people from a state of faint. (This is taken from an ancient Chassidic manuscript of unknown authorship. See also *Likkutei Sichos*, Vol. II, p. 516ff., *et al.*)

16. *Pri Etz Chayim*, Section 18, ch. 3; *Shaar HaKavannos*, the concept of immersion on Friday.

17. 250:1.

18. 250:8.

merit life").[19] Similarly, when seeing the entire span of the six millennia as six days,[20] the last generations before the coming of *Mashiach* can be understood as being Friday afternoon, [wee hours] before "the day which is all *Shabbos*." As such, there is drawn down a reflection (at least, a foretaste) of the revelation of *P'nimiyus HaTorah* which will be made manifest (in a consummate manner) by *Mashiach*.[21]

These two explanations (like the two explanations of Yaakov's remaining alone) reflect two extremes: According to the first explanation, *Chassidus* was revealed in the later generations because of their lower level. Because of the great spiritual darkness prevalent in these generations, it is necessary that there be a revelation of the higher light of *P'nimiyus HaTorah*.

According to the second explanation, by contrast, the revelation of *Chassidus* in these later generations is a reflection of the unique positive nature of the present time; it is Friday afternoon, and one can already appreciate a foreshadowing of the revelations of the era of *Mashiach!*[22]

III. To explain the above: As is well known,[23] *Yud-Tes* Kislev marks the beginning of the fundamental efforts to "spread

---

19. *Pri Etz Chayim, Shaar HaKavannos, loc. cit.*
20. See the commentary of the *Ramban* to *Bereishis* 2:3.
21. See also the explanation of these subjects in *Likkutei Sichos*, Vol. I, p. 59, *et al*; and see *Likkutei Sichos*, Vol. II, p. 467ff.

    Note also the statements of the *Zohar*, Vol. I, 117a, and 118a, explained at length in the *sichos* of *Acharon Shel Pesach*, 5730 (printed in *Likkutei Sichos*, Vol. VII, p. 206ff. and as an appendix to the series of *maamarim* entitled *Yom Tov Shel Rosh HaShanah*, 5666). See also *Or HaChayim, Parshas Tzav*, 6:2, *Rambam's Iggeres Teiman*, which is quoted and explained in *Likkutei Sichos*, Vol. II, p. 588ff., *et al.*
22. Implied is not only that the teachings of *Chassidus* ("the spreading of the wellsprings outward") are a preparation for the coming of *Mashiach* (as expressed in the renowned letter of the Baal Shem Tov printed at the conclusion of the text *Ben Pores Yosef*, and in other sources), but also that at present, there exists [— and one can appreciate —] a foreshadowing of the revelations of the era of *Mashiach*.
23. *Toras Shalom*, p. 112ff.

the wellsprings [of *Chassidus*] outward," the dissemination of the teachings of *Chassidus* to all Jews, even those found in the outer reaches.[24]

As explained on several occasions,[25] the expression "when the wellsprings spread outward," implies that the wellsprings themselves will come into these peripheries. The intent is not merely that the wellsprings [of *Chassidus*] will have an effect on distant places (and yet, these wellsprings will remain in their natural places), but that the wellsprings themselves will reach the peripheries.[26]

Furthermore, the wellsprings will *spread* in the outer reaches, i.e., they will flourish and prosper, to the extent that every dimension of the outer reaches will be permeated by the wellsprings of *Chassidus*.

Every matter has its source in the Torah. Thus the spreading of the wellsprings of *Chassidus* outward, the revelation and dissemination of *P'nimiyus HaTorah* to Jews who are found in the outer peripheries begins from [a parallel initiative within the realm of Torah study]: that *P'nimiyus HaTorah* will be revealed within the teachings of *Nigleh*, the revealed dimension of Torah law, to the extent that they are joined in absolute unity.

Before the Alter Rebbe, there were also Torah giants who achieved prominence in both *Nigleh* and *Nistar,* the Torah's mystic secrets. Obviously, their involvement in the Torah's mystic secrets transformed their approach to *Nigleh*. Nevertheless, they would regard [these disciplines] as two different realms: the revealed and the hidden.

[Against this background,] the Alter Rebbe brought about a new development, joining together both aspects of the Torah in complete unity.[27]

---

24. *Ibid.*, p. 113.
25. See *Likkutei Sichos,* Vol. X, p. 106, *et al.*
26. See *Sefer HaSichos 5704*, p. 106.
27. See the discussion of these matters in *Likkutei Sichos,* Vol. VI, p. 37; Vol. XVI, p. 38ff., *et al.*

IV. "Israel attaches itself to the Torah";[28] moreover, the Torah is "our life,"[29] and Israel and the Torah are one. It is thus evident that just as the spreading of the wellsprings outward brought about a new development in the Torah — the unification of the hidden and revealed aspects of the Torah; so, too, [it brought about a new development] within (the spiritual makeup of) the Jewish people. Through the revelation of the teachings of *Chassidus*, [the possibility was generated for] the wellsprings to spread outward within [the individual world of every] person,[30] i.e., the hidden dimensions of the soul could be united with the revealed and conscious ones.[31]

[Within each one of us, there exist dimensions of the soul which are hidden, i.e., transcendent spiritual potentials that are too elevated to be controlled by our conscious minds; for example, the power of *emunah*, faith.] It is true that before the revelation of the teachings of *Chassidus*, the light of faith, (the hidden dimension of the soul) that transcends intellect, also had an effect on the revealed powers of the soul, causing the powers of intellect and emotion to function in a different [and more elevated] fashion. Nevertheless, the power of faith itself remained higher than intellect; ([it was not] revealed [within or able to be controlled by a person's conscious self]).

The Alter Rebbe made it possible for faith and *kabbalas ol* (the acceptance of G-d's yoke) which transcend intellect to permeate an individual's personality entirely to the extent that they themselves enter [that limited] realm and become one with the person's power of conscious thought.

---

28. See the *Zohar*, Vol. III, p. 73a; see also *Likkutei Torah, Devarim*, p. 46a, *et al.*
29. [Cf. *Devarim* 32:47; the *Maariv* prayers, *Siddur Tehillat HaShem*, p. 107, *et al.*]
30. See the explanations of these concepts in *Likkutei Sichos*, Vol. X, p. 102ff.
31. See the detailed explanation of this concept in *Likkutei Sichos, ibid.*, which speaks of a more general concept, that "the wellsprings" refer to the soul and "the outer reaches" refer to the body.

Concepts that are beyond the scope of intellect become real and manifest within his mind.[32]

V. Just as on the individual level, *Chassidus* grants the potential for "spreading the wellsprings outward," that the wellsprings of the soul, [the powers of faith and *kabbalas ol*,] will be united with the outer reaches, [i.e., our conscious powers of intellect and emotion]; so, too, it grants the potential for true unity among the Jewish people, that they join as "one complete organism."[33]

The "leaders of the thousands among Israel" are the "heads and the minds" of the Jewish people;[34] they are the "wellsprings." In previous generations (before the revelation of *Chassidus*), the spiritual leaders of the Jewish people remained secluded from the people at large. Certainly, they exercised influence over the people — through the Torah that they taught them, or through the personal example of refined conduct which they demonstrated. Nevertheless,

---

32. [Trans. Note: Frequently, it is explained that the Baal Shem Tov ignited the essential spark of the Jewish soul that transcends intellect, and the Alter Rebbe contributed an intellectual dimension, communicating those teachings in *Chabad*, "wisdom, understanding, and knowledge."

The intent is not that the Alter Rebbe took ordinarily mortal intellect and used it to explain the teachings of the Baal Shem Tov, but rather that he took the teachings of the Baal Shem Tov that transcend intellect and used them to expand and reshape the nature of our thought processes, enabling them to internalize concepts that are essentially above intellect.

To illustrate by analogy: When a person feels that his life is in danger, he will run faster and jump further than the greatest athletes. Why? Because his essential desire to live has been touched. That essential desire is unlimited and it has the potential to endow each of a person's particular powers with a dimension of its unlimited power.

To apply these concepts in the analogue: A Jewish soul is "an actual part of G-d" (*Tanya*, ch. 2), unlimited and unbounded as He is. This unlimited potential is expressed in the power of faith which takes a person beyond his individual identity. The Baal Shem Tov and the Alter Rebbe showed a path of Divine service that enables faith to expand the scope of intellect. Just as the essential desire to live contributes an unlimited dimension to a person's physical prowess, so too, tapping the essential point of the soul introduces a dimension of infinity into our thought processes.]

33. See *Likkutei Torah*, the beginning of *Parshas Nitzavim*, and other sources.

34. *Tanya*, ch. 2.

although they were able to affect the Jewish people as a whole (and many individuals on a personal level), they themselves remained separate from the "outer reaches."

The new [inspiration] of "spreading the wellsprings outward" [altered the nature of this interaction], bringing the leaders of the Jewish people out from their own secluded spheres[35] and into [contact with the people at large, including those on] the peripheries. [The leaders] interacted with "the poor of their people" — with poverty understood in terms of our Sages' statement:[36] "No one is poor except in knowledge" — and spoke to them in terms that they could understand.

Moreover, since the "spreading of the wellsprings outward" must encompass every aspect and particular of these peripheries, [the involvement of] the spiritual leaders of the Jewish people [with the people at large] also included immersing themselves in the material concerns of the Jewish people.

VI. The Torah is the soul of the world, as evident from our Sages' statement[37] that the world was created "for the sake of the Torah which is called 'first.'" It can thus be concluded that since Yud-Tes Kislev brought about a new development in the Torah, it also brought about a similar new development in the world at large.

To explain: As is well known, because of [the concealment that characterizes] our world, we can appreciate only the Divine light that enclothes itself in the world, [the light originating in] the name Elokim[38] (which is numerically

---

35. See Sefer HaSichos 5700 (p. 111ff., quoted in HaYom Yom, entry 22 Iyar): "It used to be that the teacher — the Rosh Yeshivah or the Gaon — was 'alone,' and the students were 'alone.' Through the path of Chassidus which the Rebbe founded... the Rebbe is not alone, and the chassidim are not alone."
36. Nedarim 41a.
37. Rashi, Bereishis 1:1; see also Bereishis Rabbah 1:4.
38. [Trans. Note: Both Elokim and Havayah are names that refer to G-d. As explained in the Midrash (Shmos Rabbah 3:6) and the Kabbalah, the different names of G-d refer to different manifestations of His attributes.]

equivalent to *hateva*, nature[39]). Through meditating on worldly matters, we can come to the knowledge and recognition that "there is a Master to this structure."[40] We cannot, however, appreciate the name *Havayah*[41] which transcends the nature of our world.[42]

The occurrence of miracles from time to time does reveal the name *Havayah* within our world. Nevertheless, this is not relevant to the world as it exists within its own perspective. On the contrary, this represents an upset of the natural order of the world.

Chassidus, however, made possible that G-dliness which is above the nature of the world would be revealed within the world itself. Accordingly, *Chassidus* provides explanations dependent on mortal wisdom — using examples and analogies from material entities[43] — to demonstrate that the world is at one with the G-dly light that transcends the world.

VII. It is possible to explain that this concept is explained [by allusion] in the Alter Rebbe's wording in his renowned letter[44] in which he states that the redemption of *Yud-Tes Kislev* occurred in a manner in which "G-d performed wonders and manifested [His] greatness within the earth."[45]

---

39. *Pardes, Shaar* 12, ch. 2; *Tanya, Shaar HaYichud VehaEmunah*, ch. 6.
40. Cf. *Bereishis Rabbah*, the beginning of *Parshas Lech Lecha*.
41. [Trans. Note: The name *Havayah* refers to G-d's name ה-ו-ה-י, which, because of its great holiness, is not pronounced in the ordinary manner.]
42. Thus the faith of the non-Jews centers on the aspect of G-d which permeates the world, [the level of *memalei kol almin*]. See the explanations of this concept in *Sefer HaArochim-Chabad*, Vol. II, entry *Umos HaOlam*, sec. 2.
43. See the *maamar* entitled *Matzah Zu 5707*, sec. 2, *et al.* See also *Tanya*, ch. 33 which states: "As is stated in another source, *a material analogy* to this concept...."
44. Printed in *Beis Rebbe*, Vol. I, ch. 18, *Sefer HaToldos Admur HaZakein*, p. 218 [5746 edition, Vol. III, p. 720].
45. In *Beis Rebbe*, the wording cited is: "G-d performed wonders and manifested [His] greatness within the earth, for G-d manifested His greatness and performed wonders within the earth, for G-d performed wonders and manifested [His] greatness within the earth."

There are two general approaches within the order with which G-d controls the world:

a) the natural order, in which G-d's life-energy is not overtly obvious; this manner of expression stems from the name *Elokim;*

b) Divine Providence which is overtly revealed; within the natural order, it becomes obvious that the Divine light and life-energy is directed through His providence; this manner of expression stems from the name *Havayah.*[46]

Within the manner of expression that stems from the name *Havayah* itself, there are several different modes:[46]

a) a diminutive expression (*katnus*): within the *natural order,* G-d's providence can be appreciated;

b) a prominent expression (*gadlus*): G-d's providence which transcends the natural order is expressed in a manner in which its greatness is realized and appreciated, reflecting our Sages' statement:[47] "A *great matter* — "[the mystic secrets of] the Divine chariot."

Even when [G-d's providence] is expressed in a manner of *gadlus,* it is, however, relative to the expression of *katnus,* i.e., in both instances we are speaking of the manifestation of G-dliness within the context of the natural order. [In some instances, the providence is not noteworthy.] On other occasions, it will be prominent, and at times, its prominence will be staggering. [There will, however, always be a common denominator]; it is not beyond the natural order entirely.

---

46. See the *maamar* entitled *Tzohar Taaseh 5673, et al.*
47. *Sukkah* 28a.
       See also *Rambam, Mishneh Torah, Hilchos Yesodei HaTorah,* the conclusion of ch. 4, which refers to "a small matter, the differences of opinion between Abbaye and Ravva... [which are necessary] for the stabilization of this world." [It can be inferred that "greatness" refers to revelations of G-dliness which transcend the natural order.]

There is, however, another mode of expression, "G-d performed wonders," which is *entirely beyond* the natural order.[48]

VIII. These three forms of expression of [the influence from] the name *Havayah* are reflected in three types of miracles:[49]

a) Miracles which are enclothed within the natural order to the extent that the miraculous nature of the event is not obvious (like the Purim miracle). Although this is an expression of [influence from] the name *Havayah,* since the Divine Providence is not openly apparent, this can be considered as *katnus,* diminutive, as explained above.

b) Miracles which are overtly revealed, but which have an attachment to nature, for example, the conquest of Jericho by Joshua. After the miracle of the wall falling — a miracle which was not enclothed in the natural order, "the people arose... and destroyed everything that was in the city... by the edge of the sword."[50] [The fact that an actual battle was necessary indicates] an attachment to the natural order.

Or to cite another example: the war against Midian. Although the Jews had to "Select men from yourselves for the army,"[51] and "they marched against Midian,"[52] [fighting an actual war,] "not one man was missing."[53] This is obviously beyond the ordinary pattern of war.

{Or to refer to a well-known story: Once a sick person came to the Alter Rebbe. Although all of the doctors had

---

48. See *Shaar HaEmunah,* ch. 15 (p. 29b ff.).
49. Note the *maamar* entitled *VeAtah Im Na, Parshas Ki Sissa,* 5678 [*Sefer HaMaamarim 5678,* p. 222], which explains that there are levels of gradation even within the miracles that transcend nature.
50. *Yehoshua* 6:20-21.
51. *Bamidbar* 31:3.
52. *Ibid.*:7
53. *Ibid.* 49.

already despaired of healing him, the Alter Rebbe told him
to eat half of a *shemurah matzah* with water. [He followed
this directive] and regained his health.

On the surface, the story is a contradiction in terms:
[The Alter Rebbe did not merely pray for the man; he gave a
directive] to perform an act which affected the body of the
sick person and strengthened his health. On the other hand,
according to the natural order, *shemurah matzah* and water
cannot provide a remedy for a sick person ([particularly,
one whom] all the doctors despaired [of healing]).

[The resolution is indicated above:] The healing [came
from a source] above the natural order. It had, however, an
attachment to the natural order [and therefore, the *matzah*
and the water were necessary].}

    c) Miracles which do not have any attachment to the
       natural order, for example, the miraculous manner
       in which the armies of Sannecherib were devastated.
       At that time, King Chizkiyahu said:[54] "I will sleep in
       bed,"[55] and yet be victorious.

IX. On this basis, we can appreciate the wording used by
the Alter Rebbe cited above: "G-d performed wonders and
manifested [His] greatness within the earth." The revelation of the light of *Chassidus* on *Yud-Tes* Kislev originated not
only in a ray from the name *Havayah* (which would be
manifest in a diminutive manner within nature), nor even
in a prominent manner (reflecting *gadlus*, "greatness"), but
which nevertheless shares a connection to the natural order.
Instead, its source is "wonders" which G-d performed and
which transcend entirely the natural order.

---

54. See *Eichah Rabbah* 4:15.
55. See the *maamar* entitled *U'Bevoah Lifnei HaMelech*, 5654, which states: "I saw
stated in the name of one of the great [Sages] who taught that when a person
has a great difficulty, Heaven forbid, he should trust in G-d. He should not
even pray because of this, or perform any special activity like going to the
mikveh or the like. Instead, he should put his trust in G-d. This reflects the
quality of silence that represents awesome self-transcendence.

And yet, as the Alter Rebbe concludes, [these wonders were manifest] "within the earth." For the intent and purpose of the teachings of *Chassidus* is to bring "G‑d's wonders" — the Divine light which transcends nature — into the context of the world itself.[56]

X. The Torah itself recognizes the division into [*Nigleh*] and *P'nimiyus HaTorah*, which it calls "hidden," (i.e., according to the Torah itself, [these teachings] are not to be revealed). As is well known,[57] the potential to join these two dimensions together stems from the fact that the Alter Rebbe drew down "the essence of the Torah's inner dimensions."[58]

The distinction between the hidden and the revealed dimensions of the Torah exists only with regard to the way the Torah has been extended [for the sake of revelation within this world]. [For in this framework,] every entity is

---

56. These concepts are reflected in the continuation of the Alter Rebbe's letter in which he speaks of how G‑d's name "was magnified and sanctified in public, in particular, in the eyes of the ministers and the nations.... They all declared that (cf. *Tehillim* 118:23): "This emanated from G‑d; it is wondrous in our eyes," i.e., even the gentile nations recognized G‑d's wonders.

    This relates to another dimension of the redemption of *Yud-Tes Kislev*. As is well known, the Alter Rebbe did not desire to lessen the severity of the spiritual attributes of judgment confronting him by passing his hand over his forehead and face" (a letter of the Alter Rebbe, quoted in *Beis Rebbe*, Vol. I, ch. 21; *Sefer HaToldos Admur HaZakein*, p. 257 [5746 edition, Vol. IV, p. 1021]). Instead, [he sought to gain his freedom] through activity in natural channels.* The intent was that the gentile nations should realize that G‑d's wonders do not have to be manifest in a manner which nullifies their existence, but rather in a manner which permeates [their existence as well]. [See *Likkutei Sichos*, Vol. XXV, p. 193ff.]

---

    * Note also the diary of my revered father-in-law, the Rebbe, cited in *Sefer HaToldos Admur HaZakein*, p. 210, note 7 [5746 edition, Vol. III, p. 702].

57. See the *maamar* entitled *Padah BiShalom*, 5685 (based on the *Reshimos Devarim* [*Sefer HaMaamarim 5679*, p. 673] of the Rebbe Rashab, *Yud-Tes* Kislev, 5679). See also *Likkutei Levi Yitzchok, Igros*, p. 223; also *Kuntres Inyono Shel Toras HaChassidus*, note 40; *Likkutei Sichos*, Vol. XVI, *loc. cit.*

58. This is the wording used in the *maamar* entitled *Padah BiShalom, op. cit.* See also *Kuntres Inyono Shel Toras HaChassidus* which explains that the intent of the teachings of *Chassidus* is the revelation of the level of *yechidah*, which is the essence of the Torah. See the explanation in that source at length.

structured in a particular fashion. [And to relate to this
framework, the Torah also takes on several structures, each
one defined by its own rules.] The essence of the Torah
("the essence of the Torah's inner dimensions") knows no
division or definition. The essence of the Torah is the
essence of both the hidden and the revealed dimensions of
the Torah, and therefore it can fuse the hidden and the
revealed.[59]

To cite a parallel to this concept in the realm of
Halachah: The Torah recognizes the distinction between
mitzvos which are minor and those which are more severe.
Nevertheless, there is a clear statement of *Halachah* which
says:[60]

> A person who states that the Torah does not origi-
> nate from G-d — even if he says that Moshe said one
> verse or one word on his own initiative — is consid-
> ered as one who denies the Torah. The same applies
> to one who denies [the Torah's] interpretation, the
> Oral Law.

[For every aspect of the Torah —] it makes no difference
which word or which interpretation — [is an expression of
the Torah's fundamental G-dly core].

XI. Similar concepts apply with regard to the Jewish people.[61] (For as explained in sections IV-V, *Yud-Tes* Kislev

---

59. [Trans. Note: Our world is characterized by form and definition. Every entity
has a specific structure and makeup. Since the Torah served as the blueprint
into which G-d looked when He created the world (*Bereishis Rabbah* beginning
of *Bereishis*), it follows that the Torah which relates to this world is also characterized by form and definition. At this level, each discipline of the Torah is
unique and separate from the others.

    The essence of the Torah transcends these definitions, and when it is ex-
pressed, all differences become obscured. The different modes of expression
appear as complementary qualities, which can be used interchangeably without concern for the structures that would ordinarily separate one discipline
from another (See *Kuntres Inyono Shel Toras HaChassidus*, sec. 2.)]

60. *Rambam, Mishneh Torah, Hilchos Teshuvah* 3:8.

61. See the letter of the Rebbe Rashab (printed in *Kuntres U'Mayon*, p. 17 and in
HaYom Yom, p. 4) which states that *Chassidus* is intended: "to draw down the

brought about unity between the hidden and revealed dimensions of the soul.) The revelation of the teachings of *Chassidus* — which drew down the essence of the inner dimensions of the Torah — inspired the revelation of the essence of the soul,[62] the level of *yechidah*. This is why it was able to unite the hidden and revealed dimensions of the soul.

To apply this concept within the realm of our Divine service: Faith and *kabbalas ol* have the potential to permeate a person's conscious powers, because the revelation of the essence of the soul also involves the revelation of all of a person's potentials (and thus permeates them all).[63]

{Similarly, with regard to the Jewish people as a whole, *Yud-Tes* Kislev was able to generate the power which brought the "heads of the thousands of Israel" close — [not only from the perspective of their inner feelings, but] also on a revealed level — and indeed, in unity with the Jewish people as a whole. This came as a result of the revelation of the general *yechidah* for the Jewish people as a whole. At this level, [the Jewish people,] who are described with the anal-

---

depth and the inner dimension of G-d's Torah and *mitzvos* from the inner dimension and essence of *Or Ein Sof* to the inner dimension of our souls." See also note 66.

62. See *Sefer HaSichos 5703* (p. 59 and the sources cited) which states that "The *Tanya* is the Written Torah of the teachings of *Chabad Chassidus*. The name *Tanya* (תניא) uses the same letters as the word איתן, meaning 'man of strength.' *Tanya* arouses the level of איתן within the soul."

63. See *Likkutei Sichos*, Vol. VIII, p. 131ff. (with regard to the concept that the letters of the Ten Commandments were hewn from side to side in the tablets), see also *ibid.*, p. 5.

[Trans. Note: As the soul descends to this world, it takes on certain forms and definitions, reflecting those present within the world at large. At this point, the distinctions between *kabbalas ol* and faith, which represent unlimited energies and the soul's conscious powers, are relevant. With regard to the essence of the soul, by contrast, these differences do not exist. Moreover, the revelation of the essence of the soul establishes harmony and unity between the unlimited powers of the soul and its conscious powers, enabling them to work together.]

ogy of a human body, are united on the level of *yachid*,[64]
"singular oneness."[65]}

A parallel to this concept exists in the world at large[66]
(as explained in section VI). From the perspective of
revealed Divine light, it is impossible for the world to be
unified in an overt manner with the Divine light which
transcends the world. Since this [transcendent] light is
defined as light and revelation, it cannot be revealed within
the context of this world [which is characterized by con-
cealment]. ([Indeed, the very word for] world, עולם, shares
the same root letters as the word העלם, meaning "concealment."[67])

---

64. See the letter of my revered father-in-law, the Rebbe *[Igros Kodesh* of the
    Rebbe Rayatz, Vol. IV, p. 299] who quotes his father, the Rebbe Rashab, as
    saying that the connection shared by a Rebbe and a chassid transcends six
    types of relationships: father and son, essence and expression, the source of
    light and light, the primeval source and the revealed, cause and effect, noth-
    ing and something. And it includes all these relationships. See also *Likkutei
    Dibburim*, Vol. I, p. 50a, *Sefer HaSichos 5700*, p. 89.
65. This is also one of the reasons why *Ahavas Yisrael* is one of the foundations of
    Chassidus. (See *Sefer HaArachim-Chabad*, Vol. I, entry *Ahavas Yisrael*, sec. 9, *et
    al*), for the true conception of the all-encompassing unity of the Jewish
    people was revealed by the teachings of *Chassidus*.
66. The concepts explained in the text explain why the spreading of the well-
    springs of *Chassidus* outward is a preparation for the coming of *Mashiach* (as
    stated above, note 22). For the coming of *Mashiach* will consummate the
    intent of creation, showing how this world is G-d's dwelling. And it will be a
    dwelling for His essence (the series of *maamarim* entitled *Yom Tov Shel Rosh
    HaShanah 5666*), p. 3.
       Since, as is well known, G-d's dwelling will be fashioned by the Jewish
    people through the medium of the Torah (*ibid.*, p. 8), it is understandable
    why — as explained above — "the spreading of the wellsprings outward"
    (the revelation of the essence in the outer reaches) which was initiated on
    Yud-Tes Kislev, brought about [a metamorphosis] with both the Torah and
    the Jewish people.
67. [Trans. Note: According to the *Kabbalah*, in order for the world to be created,
    it was necessary for G-d to perform a *tzimtzum*, a contraction of His light.
    Moreover, as the *AriZal* explains, this contraction does not involve merely a
    diminution of the Divine light, but a total retraction of the light into His
    essence. For the world which He desired to create was a world of limitation
    and definition, and as long as His transcendent light would be revealed, it
    would be impossible for such a limited framework to come into being.

It is only through G-d's essence — for He is the Ultimate of Being and contains the potential for everything —
that there exists the possibility for the existence of a *yesh*,[68]
an entity which feels itself, and for that *yesh* to be at one
with G-d in the ultimate sense of unity.[69]

XII. The new development associated with "spreading the
wellsprings outward" — that the essence ("the wellsprings") will be united with the outer reaches — is
expressed when the wellsprings enter [— and permeate —]
peripheries which can be described (using terminology

Accordingly, once the limited framework is created, it is impossible for
there to be a revelation of the transcendent light within the context of that
limited framework. For this reason, miracles — which represent a reflection
of this transcendent light — upset and overturn the natural order.

G-d's intent — as reflected in the phrase "a dwelling in the lower worlds"
— is for His essential and most transcendent light to be revealed within our
world. And the potential for this, as the *sichah* continues to explain, lies only
in His essence. For only in — and through — His essence can the opposite
thrusts, concealment and revelation, limitation and infinity, exist together.]

68. [Trans. Note: As stated in *Tanya, Iggeres HaKodesh*, Epistle 20, it is only G-d's
essence — and not any of the revealed manifestations of Divine light — that
contains the potential to bring into being an entity which has a sensation of
self.

Among the explanations of this concept is that all the revealed manifestations of Divine light are characterized by *bittul;* their existence is subsumed
entirely by the revelation of Divine light and they have no awareness of their
own identity. They are *ayin*, nothingness, rather than *yesh*. And thus it is
impossible for them to be the source for the feeling of *yesh* that characterizes
our existence.

G-d's essence, by contrast, is *yesh*, although certainly not in the self-
conscious sense of the term; He is True Being. Unlike the manifestations of
Divine light, within His essence, there is a sense of identity — *yesh* — rather
than *ayin*, nothingness. This is the source for the sense of personal identity,
yeshus, which characterizes our world.]

69. See *Likkutei Sichos*, Vol. IV, p. 1335, note 7; see also *Or HaTorah, Acharei*, Vol.
II, pp. 564-565.

[These sources explain that every other entity has a definition. As such, it
cannot be united with another entity that does not share that definition.
G-d's essence is totally undefined. And therefore it can be at one with other
entities.]

borrowed from my revered father-in-law, the Rebbe,[70]) as "an unfitting place."

For it is only because there is an essential revelation of the wellsprings[71] that it is possible for them to permeate a periphery that is not a medium for their expression, and indeed, is even unfitting and unsuitable for them.[72] For since [these wellsprings] are the essence of G-d, the Ultimate of Being, they are the essence and the ultimate of existence for all creations. And therefore they can permeate even the existence of peripheries which (within the context of their own framework) are an unfitting place [for the revelation of G-dliness].[73]

This is the connection between the two explanations of why the teachings of *Chassidus* were revealed in these later generations: a) because of the great [spiritual] darkness [which characterizes] these generations, and b) as a foretaste of the revelations of the Era of the Redemption.

The revelation of "the essence of the inner dimensions of the Torah" is expressed in the fact that it has the potential to illuminate the darkness of these later generations, and indeed, transform this darkness into light.

From the above, it is also evident why the foretaste of the teachings of *Mashiach* ([revealed] on "Friday afternoon after midday") are associated with a time in which the

---

70. See *Sichos Simchas Torah*, 5690 (*Likkutei Dibburim*, Vol. II, p. 311b).
71. See *Likkutei Sichos*, Vol. XVI, *loc. cit.*, sec. VII, and the sources cited there.
72. See the *sichos* referred to in the previous note which state (p. 328a ff.,) that [the wellsprings must reach]: "Those who... are... thrust away into the outer reaches.... We are not speaking about [them lacking only] *Chassidus*.... [They lack the observance of] *Taharas HaMishpachah, Tefillin, Shabbos, Kashrus*.... And *Mashiach* teaches that even in such peripheries, the wellsprings exist.... They possess the most precious inheritance... the essential point [of the Jewish soul] and faith...."
73. [Trans. Note: Other than G-d, there is no entity that exists independently, by virtue of itself. He is the essence and the source of all existence, even those forms of existence which appear to conflict with Him. And since He is the essence of those forms of existence, His identity can permeate and redefine them as well.]

darkness of the exile has increased, the redoubled darkness of the era of *ikvesa deMeshicha*. For it is through the illumination of the greatest[74] darkness[75] — and the transformation of that darkness to light, "and night will shine as day"[76] — that the essential power of the teachings of *Mashiach*, "the essence of the inner dimensions of the Torah," is revealed (albeit as a foretaste).

XIII. According to the above, we can appreciate the connection between the two interpretations of the verse: "And Jacob remained alone": that he remained for his jug; and that his remaining alone parallels G-d's being "exalted alone."

It is through the refinement of small utensils[77] — i.e., the refinement of lowly and insignificant objects, the ultimate of the darkness, concealment, and hiddenness[78] — that it is possible to recognize and feel the inner core of how G-d is "exalted alone." The true oneness of the Holy

---

74. See the letter of the Rebbe Rashab cited in note 15 which explains that the process resembles the increment to [the teachings of] the Torah that came about through granting the second tablets. [As our Sages explain (*Nedarim* 22b), that had our ancestors not sinned, we would only have been granted the Five *Chumashim* and the Book of *Yehoshua*. "It is because they descended from their spiritual rung that they needed an abundance of Torah, for its source is from a very high level." Thus the revelation of "an abundance of Torah" is dependent on the Jews' descent from their spiritual rung.

75. See *Pelach HaRimon* on our Torah reading (p. 94d) which state: "Dawn is an analogy for the Future Redemption which involves the light bursting through the deepest darkness."

76. Cf. *Tehillim* 139:12.

77. See the continuation of the passage in the *Talmud* (*Chulin, loc. cit.*) which explains that (Yaakov remained for the small utensils, because) the righteous cherish their money more than their bodies. For the money of the Jewish people contains sparks of holiness which are related to the source of their souls (*Kesser Shem Tov*, p, 118; *Or Torah* of the Maggid of Mezeritch, p. 101d). They cherish their money more than their bodies, because of the advantage of refining the lowest aspects of existence. For money, (i.e., their portion in the world) is lower than their bodies.

78. See the *Meorei Or*, Letter *Peh*, sec. 50 (cited in *Or HaTorah, Vayishlach*, p. 245a): "'small utensils' — sparks of the kings [of *Tohu*] who died." See also the following note.

One, blessed be He — that He is singularly unique — stems from His essence.[79] [From the perspective of His essence], the existence of entities who feel themselves as *yesh* is no contradiction to the oneness of the Holy One, blessed be He. For from the perspective of His essence, the essence of the existence of a creation [in this world] who feels himself as a *yesh* is the true *Yesh*, [the One Who Truly Is, G-d Himself].[80]

(Adapted from *Sichos Shabbos Parshas Vayishlach, 5727, Yud-Tes Kislev 5711, 5725*)

---

79. See the conclusion of the *maamarim* on this *parshah* in *Toras Chayim* (p. 56d): "This is the intent of the phrase: 'And Yaakov remained alone,' i.e., as he exists in his source in the essence of *Or Ein Sof*... [At this level,] it is within his potential to refine darkness and transform it into light."

    That text explains that "'the small utensils'... refer to the vessels of *Tohu* that fell," and that Yaakov had the potential to refine and transform them, because of his source in G-d's essence. On this basis, the connection between the revelation of *Yud-Tes* Kislev and "And Yaakov remained alone" mentioned above can be related to the contents of *Sichas Yud-Tes Kislev 5704* (cited in note 13 above) which states: "[*Yud-Tes*] Kislev shares a connection to *Parshas Vayishlach*, [for it relates to the verse (*Bereishis* 36:31): "And these are the kings who reigned..." [which is interpreted as a reference to the *Sefiros* of *Tohu*]. For *Yud-Tes* Kislev reflects the correction of the destruction of the vessels of *Tohu*.

80. See the *Biurei Zohar* of the Mitteler Rebbe, p. 43c; the *maamar* entitled *U'Lekachtem Lachem 5661*, et al.

Parshas Vayigash

Likkutei Sichos, Vol. V, p. 239ff.

I. {"There is no word in the Torah that does not possess sublime [mystic] secrets and paths [of conduct] for men to follow."[1]} For this reason, the Torah relates [many details] concerning [the story of] Yosef and his brothers. Among the concepts [from which we can learn] is the fact that Yosef provided sustenance for his brothers and their households, as it is written:[2] "And Yosef nurtured... his brothers... [granting them] bread according to [the needs of] their children."

The concept that Yosef provided nurture for his brothers is so important that because of this, the Jews as a people are referred to with the name Yosef for all time, as it is written:[3] "He leads Yosef like sheep."

Explanation is required: When the Torah calls a person by a particular name, that is because that name expresses the inner meaning of the person given that particular name.[4] Every name reflects and manifests {not only particular events which happened to the person with that name,} but also his true nature, [i.e., who he really is].

---

1. *Zohar*, Vol. I, p. 201a.
2. *Bereishis* 47:12.
3. *Tehillim* 80:2. Note the commentaries of *Rashi* and *Metzudos David*.
4. See *Yoma* 83b which relates that Rabbi Meir would explain [certain aspects of people's character] based on their name. See also *Tanya, Shaar HaYichud Veha-Emunah*, ch. 1, [which relates that an object's name represents its fundamental life-energy]. See also *Teshuvos U'Biurim, Kovetz Lubavitch*, Vol. II; *Igros Kodesh* of the Rebbe, Vol. I, p. 288ff., which dwells on this concept at length.

The question thus arises: Why are the Jewish people called (for all time) with the name Yosef — because Yosef nurtured them in Egypt during the years of the famine? This occurrence is seemingly a secondary matter which is not associated with the essence of the Jewish people. It took place many years ago and for [only] a short time [in the span of our national history].[5]

Moreover, even if one will accept the supposition that Yosef's nurturing his brothers during the time of the famine is associated with the true nature of the Jewish people at all times,[6] there is still a conceptual difficulty. When we say that a name reflects the inner nature of an entity, the intent

---

5.   [Less than two years, according to *Rashi*.]
6.   For example, [Yishmael's daughter Bosmas] is described as "the sister of Nevios,"* because he arranged her marriage (*Rashi, Bereishis* 36:3). Since marriage is a fundamental element of a person's life, even after marriage, she is referred to in this manner.

Nevertheless, this instance cannot be compared to the case at hand because {a) [Bosmas] was not called Nevios. She was called "the sister of Nevios." For although marriage is fundamental to a person, her marriage was only arranged by Nevios, it does not reflect Nevios himself. (See the explanation later in the text why, for this reason, it is difficult to understand why the Jews are called Yosef.) [and,]}

b) the phrase "the sister of Nevios" is used to describe Bosmas, while [the Jews are not referred to as "the family of Yosef," but] are instead named Yosef.

---

*   The fact that the Torah refers to Shimon and Levi as "the brothers of Dinah" [in one verse] because they risked their lives for her sake (*Rashi, Bereishis* 34:25), is not relevant in this context. For there the Torah is obviously speaking about a specific instance: "They took their swords... and they rescued Dinah." In contrast, the Jewish people are called Yosef even afterwards, [years] after he [ceased to nurture them]. Similarly, [Bosmas] was called "the sister of Nevios" [even after her wedding].

One might say that the term "the sister of Nevios" is also used only in the context of Esav's marrying [Bosmas]. [There is, however, a distinction.] Esav's marriage is first mentioned in *Parshas Toldos*, [Bosmas is described as "the sister of Nevios" later] in *Parshas Vayishlach*. [Moreover, the emphasis is not on the wedding *per se*,] but rather on the description of Esav's descendants. (See *Likkutei Sichos*, Vol. V, p. 164.)]

See also *Rashi's* commentary to *Shmos* 15:20 [which speaks about the description of Miriam as "Aharon's sister"]. This is not the place for further discussion of this matter.

is {not that the name communicates factors that come about as a result of the nature which that name expresses}, but that the name itself expresses the nature of the named entity. This does not seem to apply with regard to the name Yosef, for although Yosef sustained the Jewish people, he was not their sustenance. Therefore even if this sustenance is associated with the inner nature of the Jewish people, it is not appropriate to call the Jews Yosef, when their sustenance {only came via Yosef, but} was not itself Yosef.

II. The above matters can be resolved through the preface of the inner meaning of the concept of the eternality of the Torah. The intent is not merely that the *mitzvos* of the Torah (given by G-d at Sinai) are [everlasting], to be observed when required for all time without change, neither adding to them or detracting from them.[7] Instead, the intent is that the commands themselves are everlasting.[8] This is the intent of the verses: "The word of our G-d will endure forever,"[9] and "His words are living and enduring... forever."[10] G-d's words (which are written in the Torah[11]) are themselves eternal and endure forever. [12]

---

7. *Rambam, Mishneh Torah, Hilchos Yesodei HaTorah* 9:1; the ninth of the *Rambam's* "Thirteen Principles of Faith" (Commentary to the *Mishnah, Sanhedrin,* ch. 10); Introduction to *Pirush HaMishnayos* of the *Rambam.*

8. To use the wording of the Rogatchover Gaon: "It is a factor that is drawn down continuously and [is always] active" (*Tzafnas Paneach, Makkos* 11a; *Tzafnas Paneach LiHilchos Terumos,* Vol. I, p. 120), see also *Likkutei Sichos,* Vol. VIII, p. 151.

9. *Yeshayahu* 40:8.

10. Daily liturgy (*Siddur Tehillat HaShem,* p. 48).

11. The commentary of the *Radak* (and similarly, *Metzudas David*) to *Yeshayahu, loc. cit.* states: "'The word of our G-d' which He spoke through His prophets." (This appears to include words of prophecy that are not written in the Torah.) *Tanya,* ch. 25 (p. 32a) quotes this verse with regard to the revelation of His will through His speech, i.e., the Torah." This appears to indicate that this also refers to the Oral Law. {For the essential revelation of G-d's will which was spoken is in the Oral Law, (*Tanya, Iggeres HaKodesh,* Epistle 29). See the following note.}

12. It can be understood from the *Tanya's* statement that the reason the unity with G-d established through [the performance of] the *mitzvos* "is everlast-

This is the inner reason why the *mitzvos* of the Torah will never be changed. For since "the word of our G-d will endure forever," and "His words are living and enduring... forever," therefore, "He will not change[13]... or modify His faith forever."[14]

III. The concept that applies to the *mitzvos* of the Torah also applies to the stories of the Torah. Their eternality is not only expressed in the fact that they contain lessons which can be derived by every Jew in every generation. Instead, the very fact that the stories contain continuously relevant lessons comes about because the stories themselves are — as they exist in the spiritual sphere — ongoing.[15]

Similarly, Jews from every generation can [certainly] learn lessons from the story of Yosef providing food for [the Jewish people]. For example, the (fundamental[16]) [lesson] is reflected in the *Zohar's* [insight] cited by the Alter Rebbe in *Tanya*[17] that Yosef showered goodness upon his brothers[18] despite what they had done to him. Similarly, every person should emulate his example; instead of retaliating against a

---

ing," is that "the revelation of His will through His speech, which is the Torah, is everlasting."*

---

*   See also the beginning of *Shaar HaYichud VehaEmunah* which explains that "The word of our G-d will endure forever," and "His words are living and enduring... forever," is that the words and letters (of [His] speech) themselves stand and endure forever.

13. The hymn *Yigdal.*

14. This is also evident from the statements of the *Tanya*, ch. 25, which associate the fact that the *mitzvos* are unchanging with the phrases: "The word of our G-d will endure forever," and "His words are living and enduring... forever."

15. A further point is evident from the *Tzafnas Paneach (loc. cit.)* that since the Torah relates the story (*Shmos* 2:21) that Moshe took an oath to Yisro, that oath is a continuously active force. Even in the present age (although the oath was absolved), it is still a relevant force. [See *Nedarim* 10a-b.]

16. Indeed, [when speaking about the narrative,] the *Zohar*, Vol. I, p. 201a,b cites only this lesson.

17. The conclusion of ch. 12.

18. The fact that at the outset, he caused them some hardship is explained in *Or HaTorah, Mikeitz*, p. 340b ff.

person who did him harm, he should "repay those who are culpable with goodness."

Over and above this and any other lessons that can be derived from the story, the fact that Yosef sustained his brothers during the famine remains an ongoing event in the spiritual realms.

IV. Another point must be mentioned with regard to the lessons and directives that can be derived from the Torah. Whenever we derive a law or a directive from a particular Torah concept, [the context is also significant]. Nothing concerning the Torah is merely coincidental. On the contrary, everything is very precise. Therefore the fact that [the Torah] has ordained that this law or directive be derived from this concept is proof that this concept is the rationale or source for this particular law or directive.

To apply this concept to the subject at hand: [Two concepts] can be derived from the fact that the Torah ordained that the concept of "repay[ing] those who are culpable with goodness" from a) Yosef and b) his [efforts] to sustain his brothers during the years of famine:

a) The potential for every Jew to "repay those who are culpable with goodness" is granted to him[19] by Yosef.[20] This

---

19. [The fact that every Jew receives influence from Yosef raises a question, for] *Torah Or,* beginning of *Parshas Va'eira,* states that "we call only three — Avraham, Yitzchak, and Yaakov — Patriarchs" (*Berachos* 16b) because "the attributes of the Patriarchs alone must be present within every individual, for they are the root and source of the entire Jewish people." With regard to the tribes, by contrast, "there are individuals who do not possess these qualities at all."

This, however, does not represent a contradiction to the above, because Yosef is "the potential which brings the essential influence of Yaakov into revelation among the recipients"; "all of the offspring of Yaakov are brought into revelation by Yosef" (*Biurei HaZohar LeAdmur HaEmtzaei,* p. 30a). Thus since the attribute of Yaakov is possessed by each individual (see note 23), and this attribute is brought out by Yosef, every person must also possess an attribute of Yosef.

Nevertheless, it is still appropriate to say that "we call only three — Patriarchs." For the influence of Yosef that every person must possess is {not the

attribute is identified with Yosef and it is within the power of every Jew to emulate it because of the influence Yosef grants him.

b) The potential which [Yosef grants] was conveyed by sustaining the Jewish people in the years of famine. By giving nurture to his brothers, he granted them (not only food in a material sense, but also) [his own] potential and positive [spiritual] quality.[21] This empowered them (and their descendants in all the generations to come) to sustain other Jews in the manner which Yosef did, to "repay those who are culpable with goodness."

On this basis, we can appreciate why Jews are continually referred to with the name Yosef, because he sustained and nurtured them during the years of famine: The positive attribute of "repaying those who are culpable with goodness" is a fundamental quality which relates to the very essence of the Jews (as will be explained in sec. XIII). Since this attribute is identified with Yosef (and is drawn down to

---

attribute of Yosef himself (— that quality is indeed possessed only by those who are from the tribes of Ephraim and Menasheh* —), but} is the power which communicates influence from Yaakov.

See sec. XII which explains that the attribute to "repay those who are culpable with goodness" stems from Yosef, for he is the one who draws down the essence of the soul (as it exists within the realm of *Atzilus*), i.e., the level of Yaakov, even to those who are culpable.

* It must be noted [that there is a certain universal quality] to Ephraim and Menasheh as well, as reflected in the fact that the entire Jewish people are blessed: "May G-d make you as Ephraim and Menasheh," as *Bereishis* 48:20 states (see *Targum ben Uziel*): "Through you, (Yosef my son) Israel will be blessed."

20. On this basis, we can appreciate our Sages' statement (*Pirkei d'R. Eliezer*, ch. 39) that Yosef was also called כלכל, as it is written: ויכלכל יוסף, "And Yosef nurtured."

21. [This quality is referred to] as the attribute of the Holy One, blessed be He, who "repays those who are culpable with goodness." ([For this reason, G-d is praised in this manner in] *Bircas HaGomel*; see the comments of the *Rif* to *Berachos*, the beginning of ch. 9.)

every Jew because Yosef is continually nurturing his broth-ers[22]), the Jewish people as a whole are called Yosef.

From the fact that the primary names for the Jewish people are Yisrael and Yaakov, it is obvious that their prin-cipal qualities stem from receiving the influence of these names.[23] Nevertheless, there are several qualities which express the fundamental nature of a Jew. In the verse, "He leads Yosef like sheep," what is relevant is the quality which the Jews receive from Yosef.

V. To offer greater explanation to the above, it is necessary to preface the interpretation of the *Midrash* on the verse: "He leads Yosef like sheep." (Not only is the intent of the verse that G-d leads the Jewish people who are called Yosef, but also that) G-d should relate to the Jewish people in the manner exemplified by Yosef. To quote the *Midrash*:[24]

> Yosef brought [grain] from the years of plenty to the years of famine, so, too, bring us from the life of this world to the life of the World to Come.[25]

> Yosef sustained each person according to his deeds, as it is written:[26] "And Yosef sustained his father...." For us as well, sustain us according to our deeds.

---

22. [Trans. Note: For as stated above, every story in the Torah is a reflection of an ongoing spiritual pattern.]

23. The reason why although every Jew must possess the spiritual qualities of all three Patriarchs, the Jewish people share a greater connection with Yaakov than with Avraham and Yitzchak, is explained in *Likkutei Sichos*, Vol. III, p. 787ff.; Vol. IV, p. 1051, note 18.

24. *Yalkut Shimoni* on the verse from *Tehillim* cited above.

25. [Trans. Note: In this *sichah*, the term, the World to Come, is used to refer to the Era of the Redemption and more particularly, the Era of the Resurrection. Although there are sources which apply this term to *Gan Eden*, the non-corpo-real world of souls, in *Chassidus*, it is used primarily in the context mentioned here. See the *maamar* entitled *Kol Yisrael Yesh La'Hem Cheilek L'Olam HaBah* translated in *Anticipating the Redemption*, Vol. I, p. 40ff., which discusses this subject.]

26. *Bereishis* 47:12. This is the wording in the passage from the *Yalkut Shimoni* cited above. Seemingly, the focus of the *Midrash* is also on the conclusion of

Rabbi Menachem said in the name of Rabbi Avin:
"Just as Yosef acted generously with his brothers
although they brought evil upon him, so, too,
although we have brought evil upon You, act generously with us."

This passage raises several questions:

a) It is obvious that had not Yosef collected and
protected the grain which grew in the years of plenty, as it
is written:[27] "And he gathered all the food of the seven
years... and collected it," it would have been lost entirely,
and would have been of no use later. With regard to the
good deeds that the Jewish people perform in this world, it
is seemingly not appropriate to say that they will be lost.
Why then is it necessary for there to be a special request:
that G-d "bring us from the life of this world to the life of
the World to Come"?

b) Our Sages describe our world as an "antechamber,"
and the World to Come as "the hall."[28] [In the analogy, it
appears that] this world is described as "the years of
plenty" and the World to Come as "the years of famine."
How is that appropriate? On the contrary, this world is
merely "an antechamber" for the World to Come.

c) Yosef's greatness is (— as this *Midrash* itself quotes
Rabbi Menachem who said it in the name of Rabbi Avin —)
that he acted generously with his brothers despite the fact
that they brought evil upon him. Thus he did not "sustain
them according to their deeds," why then does the *Midrash*
use this expression to describe Yosef's positive attributes
(instead of saying "according to their needs")?

---

the verse. See also the *Midrash Tehillim* (Buber edition) on the verse. That
text, however, differs from the text of the *Yalkut* in several particulars.

The text in the *Yalkut HaMachiri* reads: "Yosef sustained his brothers
according to their deeds, as it is written: 'bread according to [the needs of]
their children,' so too, sustain us according to our deeds." According to this
version, the emphasis is on his sustaining his brothers.

27. *Bereishis* 41:48-49.
28. *Avos* 4:16.

d) Were we to ask G-d to take notice of our deeds, we could appreciate that this is a new development. "Sustaining us according to our deeds," however, does not appear to be a new matter. On the contrary, fairness would require that everyone be requited according to his deeds. What is the necessity for a special request that G-d "sustain us according to our deeds" and why must we reinforce this request by citing Yosef's example?[29]

VI. [These questions can be resolved through the explanation of a fundamental concept which applies to *mitzvos*.] As mentioned on several occasions, *mitzvos* are not an intermediary which leads to another purpose. Instead, the purpose is within [the mitzvos] themselves. For the [Divine] will for *mitzvos* is rooted in G-d's essence itself (as it is said:[30] "All of the *mitzvos* relate to G-d's essence"). And with regard to G-d's essence (and His will), it is not appropriate to say that it exists for a purpose outside itself.

Based on this concept, the Alter Rebbe explains[31] the statement of the *Mishnah:*[32] "One moment of *teshuvah* and good deeds in this world is more desirable than the entire life of the World to Come." The World to Come is the reward given for Divine service in this world, and seemingly, the reward should be greater than the service

---

29. See the *maamar* entitled *Agura BiOholecho Olamim 5695*, sec. 3 (and the sources cited there) and the interpretation of the verse (*Tehillim* 62:13): "And kindness is Yours, O G-d, for You reward each man according to his deeds." {There a similar question is raised: What "kindness" is it to "reward each man according to his deeds?" Note the resolution offered there. See also the explanation given in sec. 1 of that source based on the *Ikkarim*.}

The interpretation offered in that source is not appropriate to explain the request "sustain us according to our deeds." For seemingly, a request is not necessary for this. In particular, this applies because the psalms of *Tehillim* are continuous requests {for this reflects the ordinary pattern that results from G-d's kindness}. Certainly, there is no need to preface the matter by citing Yosef's example.

30. See *Toras Shalom*, p. 190ff.

31. *Likkutei Torah, Devarim* 28d ff.

32. *Avos* 4:17.

performed to attain it. Indeed, the *Mishnah*[31] itself states: "One moment of pleasure in the World to Come is greater than the entire life of this world."

[The explanation is] that the purpose of man's creation is {not for man himself, but}as the *Mishnah* states:[33] "I was created solely to serve my Creator." This purpose is achieved through the observance of *mitzvos* in this world. [This alone is the *raison d'être* for man and for the entire creation.] Nevertheless, because "the Holy One, blessed be He, does not withhold reward from any created being,"[34] a person who has brought this purpose to fruition is deserving of an unlimited reward. And thus in the World to Come, a person receives a revelation of the pleasure which he drew down through the observance of *mitzvos* in this world.

The person will experience the revelation of this pleasure in the World to Come. For this reason, we are told that: "One moment of pleasure in the World to Come is greater than the entire life of this world." It is clear, however, that the revelation of this pleasure (to a mortal) — the reward for the *mitzvah* — cannot be compared to the essence of the pleasure (experienced by G-d, as it were) which is the essence of the *mitzvah* performed in this world.

To restate the concept using different wording:[35] The reward for the *mitzvah*, the World to Come, reflects the pleasure and the satisfaction of a created being, while the pleasure and satisfaction of G-d comes, as it were, from the actual performance of the *mitzvos*. Since there is no comparison between a created being and the Creator, it is clear that "the entire life of the World to Come," the satisfaction experienced by mortals, cannot be compared with "*teshuvah*

---

33. The conclusion of Tractate *Kiddushin*.
34. *Mechilta, Rashi,* commenting on *Shmos* 22:30. Our Sages conclude: "And if this holds true for an animal, certainly, He will not withhold the reward due a human."
35. See the series of *maamarim* entitled *VeKachah 5637,* ch. 12.

and good deeds in this world," the satisfaction experienced by the Creator.

VII. Based on the above, the following points require explanation:

a) The World to Come represents merely the satisfaction to be experienced by a created being. This cannot be compared to the *mitzvah* itself, the satisfaction experienced by G-d. Hence, it would appear that, by giving them the World to Come, G-d has not rewarded the Jews fairly for their observance of the *mitzvos*.

b) The fact that the World to Come follows this world indicates that (the matters of this world including) the intent of the observance of the *mitzvos* will be consummated only in the World to Come. {As the Alter Rebbe states in *Tanya*:[36] "The ultimate goal and the consummation of the creation[37] of this world" for which "it was originally created" is the Era of *Mashiach*,[38] and more particularly, the Era of the Resurrection.} Nevertheless, from the above explanations (sec. VI), it appears that the ultimate intent is

---

36. Ch. 36 (p. 46a).

37. It appears that the Hebrew text should read בריאת and not בריאות. This version is found in several printings of the *Tanya*.

38. With regard to "the Era of *Mashiach*," it could be explained (albeit with a somewhat forced argument), that the *mitzvos* will also be observed in that Era as well. [Hence, there is a connection to G-d's essential will also at that time.] {Our Sages' statement (*Niddah* 61b) that "In the future, [the observance of] *mitzvos* will be nullified" applies only in the Era of Resurrection, but in the Era of *Mashiach*, before the resurrection, their [observance] will not be nullified* (*Tanya, Iggeres HaKodesh*, Epistle XXVI, p. 145a).**}

Indeed, the essence of the charge "Today to perform them" and the ultimate consummation of [our] deeds will be in the Era of *Mashiach* (*Torah Or*, p. 46a ff., the series of *maamarim* entitled *VeKachah 5637*, ch. 17ff.). With regard to the Era of the Resurrection, however, the resolution offered in the text above is necessary.

---

* It appears that the Hebrew text should read בטלות and not בטלים, as we find in the previous phrase.

** See also *S'dei Chemed: K'lallim, Os Mem*, sec. 28 (Vol. III, p. 561c ff.); *Divrei Chachamim*, sec. 53 (Vol. IX, p. 1862b), *et al.*

achieved at present, through the observance of the *mitzvos*, and receiving the reward in the World to Come is a secondary factor {coming only because "the Holy One, blessed be He, does not withhold reward from any created being"} which is not relevant to the essential intent.

VIII. These points can be resolved as follows: G-d's essence is not defined; it cannot be classified as concealment or revelation. This leads to two factors:

a) Through the observance of *mitzvos* in this physical world — since this is the will of G-d's essence — one [bonds with], "takes," [as it were,] G-d's essence. Although the fact that we are now drawing down G-d's essence into this world is concealed, since He is not defined, Heaven forbid, by concealment and revelation, it is not appropriate to say that [the present] lack of revelation detracts from His essence which is being drawn down.

On the contrary, precisely for this reason, G-d's essence is drawn down in this world [and not in the World to Come]. The World to Come is characterized by revelation — and revelation is not a medium which to express G-d's essence. It is only in a place where the influence is concealed — in our material world — that His essence can be drawn down. Thus it is through the observance of *mitzvos* [in this material realm] that His essence is drawn down.[39]

---

39. See a similar concept in *Tanya*, ch. 36 (p. 45b) which states that, in contrast to our material world, the spiritual realms represent a descent from the radiance of His presence. See also the *maamar* entitled *Basi LeGani 5711*, sec. IV, and the sources cited there.

[Trans. Note: The intent appears to be that revelation, by definition, involves a specific — and therefore limited — entity. If something is revealed, it can be described and delineated and therefore has its own boundaries. Even a transcendent revelation is defined as being transcendent. Although it is unbounded by the limitations of existence as we know it, it is defined — it is not truly unbounded; it has its set scope. As such, it is not an appropriate medium for G-d's essence, for G-d's essence is entirely unbounded, knowing no limitation whatsoever. And since there is no way that a limited entity can be a medium for the expression of G-d's essence, which is totally above limi-

b) Since G-d's essence is not bound by any limitations, Heaven forbid, we cannot say that it must remain concealed.[40] Certainly, it can come into revelation (although [the ordinary channels of] revelation cannot be compared to His essence).[41]

On this basis, we can appreciate how the World to Come can serve as a fair reward for the Jews' observance of the *mitzvos* in this world. For in [the World to Come], there will be revealed, {not only the revealed level of G-dliness — [which lead to] the satisfaction experienced by a created being, but also} the satisfaction experienced by the Creator,[42] as it were, the essence which is drawn down [through our observance of the *mitzvos*] in the present era.

This revelation is necessary, (not only because "the Holy One, blessed be He, does not withhold reward from any created being," but also) because His will and His essence are drawn down through [our observance of] the *mitzvos*.[43]

---

tation, all of the revealed levels are inappropriate. It is only our world which is characterized by concealment that is a fit medium.]

40. [Trans. Note: For that would be a limitation, that His essence can only be concealed, and it cannot be revealed.]

41. [Trans. Note: When the essence is revealed, its revelation transcends the ordinary mediums for revelation. For example, when a person's life is threatened, he will run and jump in a manner which surpasses the skills of professional athletes. Because the essence of his life-energy is revealed at that time, it will be expressed in a manner which is entirely above the limits of what is normal and ordinary.]

42. See the series of *maamarim* entitled *VeKachah*, sec. XII, and sec. XV. (Sec. XII states that [in the Future, all existence] will be elevated [to G-d's essence], not that G-d's essence will be revealed.)

[Despite the fact that the World to Come will also involve the satisfaction of the Creator, G-d's essence,] it is still appropriate to say "One moment of *teshuvah* and good deeds in this world is more desirable than the entire life of the World to Come," as explained in sec. XIII of that source.

43. See also *Likkutei Sichos*, Vol. IV, p. 1054, which explains the concept of a dwelling in the lower worlds, stating that a "dwelling" is a place, {not only where the entire essence is found, but that} the essence is found in a state of revelation. [To cite an analogy: It is in a person's own home where he relaxes his constraints and reveals his personality traits without inhibition.]

Since the intent of the expression "a dwelling in the lower worlds" is a dwelling for His essence, a rung which transcends all revealed levels {for

The revelation of His essence in the World to Come will manifest this essential quality, the essence that is drawn down at present [through the performance of the *mitzvos*]. {For were it necessary that the influence drawn down at present remain concealed, that itself would be a sign that G-d's essence is not (being drawn down).[44] For with regard to G-d's essence, no limitations [— neither of concealment nor of revelation —] are appropriate, as stated above.[45]

IX. The reason why "the satisfaction of the Creator" (which is above the World to Come as it would exist on its own accord) will also be revealed to the Jews is that the Jews are one with G-d, as will be explained.

All of the other created beings are merely intermediaries [brought into being] to carry out G-d's ultimate intent. (G-d's intent is not, however, focused on them them-

---

even G-d's light, which is a revelation from His essence, [was emanated] for the sake of this purpose (the *maamar* entitled *Anochi Havayah E-lohecha 5703*, sec. 3),} it is not appropriate to say that it is a composite of two elements. Therefore, it is necessary to say that the revelation of the essence (is not incremental, but rather [intrinsic],) a [fundamental element] of G-d's essence being drawn down, as will be explained above. See also the following note.

44. On this basis, we can comprehend the statement (*Pesachim* 50b; see also *Shulchan Aruch HaRav, Hilchos Talmud Torah* 4:3, and in the *Kuntres Acharon* to that source): "A person should always occupy himself in the Torah and its *mitzvos*, even when lacking the proper intent, for from [Divine service] without the proper intent comes Divine service with the proper intent."

On the surface, since "deed is of primary importance" (*Avos* 1:17), what is the necessity for the rationale: "From [Divine service] without the proper intent comes Divine service with the proper intent"? [Seemingly, even if ultimately, the person will continue to serve G-d without the proper intentions, as long as he is performing *mitzvos*, his deeds would be acceptable.]

[The resolution is that] if [Divine service] for the proper intent would not ultimately come, there would be a lack, not only in the revelation [of G-d's essence drawn down by the Divine service], but in the drawing down of the essence itself, as evident from the previous note. [For if the person's Divine service would never reflect the proper intent, that would show that the *mitzvos* he performs are not G-dly acts. For if they are G-dly, their inner G-dliness must ultimately be revealed.]

45. See the explanation of similar concepts in *Likkutei Sichos*, Vol. IX, p. 156ff., in the interpretation of our Sages' statement (cf. *Zohar*, Vol. III, p. 5a): "When is He great? When He is in the city of our G-d."

selves).⁴⁶ Were this also to be said with regard to the Jewish
people, it would not be appropriate that they be granted a
revelation of the "satisfaction of the Creator" which transcends entirely the set of created beings." The truth,
however, is that "Israel, and the Holy One, blessed be He,
are all one."⁴⁷ Although it is said: "I was created solely to
serve my Creator," the Jews are not an intermediary [neces-
sary] for G-d's ultimate intention; His ultimate intention
encompasses them themselves.⁴⁸

{For this reason, we see that the Jews derive satisfaction
from *mitzvos* which are *chukim*. Since the observance of the
chukim is motivated by *kabbalas ol*, the acceptance of G-d's
yoke, a quality which expresses *bittul*, self-nullification, [one
may ask:] How is it possible for them to evoke vitality and
pleasure? [They appear to run contrary to a person's self-
interest.]

Nevertheless, [the Jews' mission] — "I was created
solely to serve My Creator" — which is expressed in *bittul*
and *kabbalas ol*, does not nullify the identity of a Jew. On the
contrary, this is their true identity.⁴⁹ [And therefore, the
observance of the *chukim* brings them pleasure.]}

---

46. [Trans. Note: To cite an analogy: the scenery and settings for a play. They are
important only because they create the background for the play, not because
there is an intrinsic desire for them in their own right.]

47. See the *Zohar*, Vol. III, pp. 73a and 93b. See also our Sages' interpretation of
the description (*Shir HaShirim* 5:2 of the Jewish people as "My perfect one."
[*Shir HaShirim Rabbah* renders that term as] "My twin." See also *Likkutei
Torah, Shir HaShirim*, pp. 34d, 39a).

48. See the elucidation of this concept in *Likkutei Sichos*, Vol. II, p. 604, which
explains the reason why the quote uses the expression קוני for Creator {and
not בוראי (although it uses the term נבראתי for the term "created") or the
like}. [קוני relates to the term קנין, meaning "transaction."]
       When is a transaction completed? When it involves not only the produce
[grown on land] or the benefit from [a person's] labor, [but the complete and
total transfer of an entity to another domain, to the extent that] the object no
longer exists as a separate entity, and its entire existence is encompassed by
the fact that it is owned by the person who acquired it.

49. See *Likkutei Sichos*, Vol. VIII, p. 131ff., where this concept is explained.
       [Trans. Note: When speaking within the context of a person's individual
identity and self-concern, *kabbalas ol* and *bittul* definitely demand that a

[Since the Jews are at one with G-d's essence,] they can accept "the satisfaction of the Creator" in a revealed manner.

X. The above provides us with an explanation of our Sages' comments in the *Midrash* concerning the phrase: "He leads Yosef like sheep."

First the *Midrash* states: "Yosef brought grain from the years of plenty to the years of famine; so, too, bring us from the life of this world to the life of the World to Come." [The years of famine are used as an analogy for the World to Come, because just] as grain does not grow in years of famine, [*mitzvos* as we know them will not be performed in the World to Come].

Yosef's [achievement] was that he collected the grain from the years of plenty and preserved it for the years of famine. Similarly, we ([for] all Jews are referred to as Yosef as stated in section 1) [ask G-d] to "bring us from the life of this world to the life of the World to Come." [Our request is that] the essence [of G-d], the satisfaction of the Creator, which flourishes[50] through our Divine service in this world, should also be revealed in the World to Come.

To this, the attribute of judgment will come with a complaint: The reason why the satisfaction of the Creator is revealed to the Jews in the World to Come is that (as stated in section IX) their observance of the *mitzvos* is characterized by pleasure and vitality (which in turn reflect that the Divine intent is in them, in the Jews themselves, as stated above). When, however, a Jew observes *mitzvos* without vitality {— even when he observes them with [the resolve

---

person sacrifice his self-interest and give up immediate gratification. But a person's individual identity and self-concern do not define who he is. Beyond his "I" of wants and desires, he possesses a G-dly soul which defines his true self, the core of His being. And it is *bittul* and *kabbalas ol* which give his G-dly soul expression and satisfaction.]

50. See the *maamar* entitled *HaBayim Yasrish Yaakov* and its explanation in *Torah Or*.

of] *kabbalas ol,* (but without the vitality of love and fear[51]), certainly when he performs them [merely] out of rote and habit,[52] and needless to say, when he performs the *mitzvos* with a selfish intent —} it does not appear appropriate that [such observance] would cause G-d's essence to be revealed in the World to Come. [Certainly,] "Deed is most essential,"[53] and thus even such Divine service can draw down G-d's essence. Nevertheless, when it is drawn down in such a manner, it is not at all connected to revelation.[54] And so the attribute of judgment claims: This essential influence should not be revealed in the World to Come."

To resolve this, the *Midrash* states a second request: "Yosef sustained each person according to his deeds.... For us as well, sustain us according to our deeds."

Yosef told his brothers:[55] "You thought to do me harm, [but] G-d intended it for good, to accomplish [what is before us] today, that a large nation be kept alive." Thus [— he emphasized to his brothers —] because of your deeds (although you did not have in mind the positive result that stemmed from it), I will repay you "measure for measure"; "I will sustain you and your children."[56]

---

51. See *Tanya,* the beginning of ch. 4; *Kuntres HaAvodah,* ch. 2, p. 15.

52. See *Yeshayahu* 29:13 [which states: "And your fear of Me shall be like a habitual mortal precept"]; see also *Tanya,* the conclusion of ch. 39.

53. Cf. *Avos* 1:17; see also *Torah Or,* p. 90a ff.

54. In general, revelation does not result from the deed [of the *mitzvos*] itself, but comes as a result of the love and fear [which motivate the observance of the *mitzvos*] (see *Likkutei Sichos,* Vol. III, p. 956; Vol. IV, p. 1054). Aside from this, the revelation of "the satisfaction of the Creator" (which transcends [ordinary] revelation) comes when the *kabbalas ol* which transcends intellect is drawn down within our internal powers, as stated above, sec. IX.

55. *Bereishis* 50:20.

56. *Ibid.*:21. Note the commentary of the *Or HaChayim* to the previous verse: "This can be compared to a person who desired to give a colleague a cup of deadly poison to drink, but instead, gave him wine." (The *Or HaChayim* concludes that for this reason, the person is not culpable. The same logic can, however, be used as the rationale why "I will sustain you and your children.")

Based on the above, we can also appreciate the explanation in *Tanya,* the conclusion of ch. 12, which states that "Instead of repaying [a person who

Just as Yosef sustained his brothers because of their deeds (without concern for their intent); so, too, we ask G-d to sustain us according to our deeds. We request that He view only the positive deeds which we have performed [without necessarily being concerned with their intent]. And since with regard to actual deed, "Even the sinners of Israel are filled with *mitzvos*, like a pomegranate is filled with seeds,"[57] we request that He gives us the reward mentioned above.

Indeed, it is appropriate that He grant us the reward as if the deed was performed with the appropriate intent. To cite a parallel: With regard to *tzedakah* (which is the paradigm of all *mitzvos*[58]), the *Talmud* states[59] that a person who says: "[I am giving] this *sela* to charity so that my son will

---

caused one harm] according to his deeds, one should repay those who are culpable with goodness." On the surface, one might ask: Why should goodness be granted to people who are culpable?*

[The resolution to this question is that] whatever the colleague brought upon the person ultimately stems from G-d (see *Tanya, Iggeres HaKodesh*, Epistle XXV). Since "Everything that G-d does is for the good" (*Berachos* 60b), he must repay him with good. For what he did to him was done as an agent of the Holy One, blessed be He, who decreed this for his benefit,** as was the case with regard to Yosef's brothers.*** See *Bereishis* 45:8, and the commentary of Seforno to *Bereishis* 50:19.

---

* Note *Bava Metzia* 32b which, when speaking about the *mitzvah* of unloading a fallen animal, states that when there is a choice between unloading an animal belonging to a friend and one belonging to an enemy, it is a *mitzvah* to deal with the animal belonging to one's enemy, to curb one's natural inclination. See *Shulchan Aruch HaRav, Hilchos Ovrei Derachim Vitzaar Baalei Chayim*, law 10.

** To cite a parallel, note our Sages' statement (*Bava Kamma* 92b): "The wine belongs to its owner, but the agent deserves a favor." See also *Derech Mitzvosecha, Mitzvas Milah*, sec. I, the conclusion of ch. 3; and *Likkutei Sichos*, Vol. VII, p. 14, note 22.

***On this basis, we can appreciate why the *Tanya* instructs us to learn from Yosef and his brothers. For in this instance, they saw *in an overt manner* how "G-d intended it for good." And this serves as an explanation why each person must repay the culpable with kindness.

57. *Eruvin* 19a; the conclusion of *Chagigah; Berachos* 53a which speaks of "the empty ones among you." See also *Likkutei Torah, Shir HaShirim*, p. 37a.
58. *Tanya*, ch. 37 (p. 48b).
59. *Rosh HaShanah* 4a, *Bava Basra* 10b.

live," is "a completely righteous man." Although outwardly, he is performing the *mitzvah* for a personal intent, since inwardly, his heart is directed to G-d [— for every Jew "desires to perform all the *mitzvos*"[60]], not only is the deed of *tzedakah* (itself) perfect, the deed affects the person himself, and [when examining] his inner dimensions, he is (— through this deed —) a complete *tzaddik*.

XI. Despite the above explanations, there is still room for the attribute of judgment to protest: When a Jew observes a *mitzvah*, but he does so for a personal intent, it is possible to say that the will and the inner desire of the soul can, although they are [functioning] in a hidden manner, combine and enclothe themselves within the observance of the *mitzvos*,[61] as explained in section X. When, by contrast, a person transgresses, Heaven forbid, [this motif does not seem appropriate]. It is true that through *teshuvah* (motivated by love), a person can transform his willful sins into merits,[62] and these merits will also earn a Jew a portion in the World to Come.[63] It is however, [seemingly] not appropriate, to say that these deeds were carried out with (the inner) desire of the soul.

{On the contrary, the desire of the soul is "to distance oneself from sin."[60] The reason that the person stumbled and transgressed that "his natural inclination overpowered him,"[60] [and compelled him to act] against his [own inner] will.}

---

60. *Rambam, Mishneh Torah, Hilchos Geirushin* 2:20.
61. It can be explained that this is the rationale why "[the observance of] the *mitzvos* does not require intent" (See *Berachos* 13a; *Eruvin* 95b), [i.e., that when a person observes a *mitzvah* without focusing on its intent, it is nevertheless considered as if he performed the *mitzvah*]. Even though he does not have a conscious intent, there is, nevertheless, the inner intent of his soul, as explained in *Likkutei Sichos*, Vol. IV, p. 1130. See *Tanya*, the conclusion of ch. 39. Explanation is, nevertheless, still required.
62. *Yoma* 86b.
63. *Likkutei Torah, Vayikra*, p. 26c.

Since our request to "bring us from the life of this world to the life of the World to Come" is based on the concept that the good deeds which are performed in this world are associated with the person's pleasure and will, as stated in section IX, it is difficult to understand: How is this motif appropriate with regard to the merits that come from willful transgressions that are directly opposite to the will of the soul?

To resolve this difficulty, the *Midrash* continues (introducing this as a new concept: "Rabbi Menachem[64] said) in the name of Rabbi Avin: 'Just as Yosef acted generously with his brothers although they brought evil upon him,' so, too, although we have brought evil upon You, act generously with us.'"

Yosef sustained his brothers because they performed a deed which ultimately brought about good, although beforehand, at the time of their actions, "they brought evil upon him." Similarly, [we are asking G-d]: "Although we have brought evil upon You, act generously with us." Since ultimately, from the "evil we have brought upon You," will come good, because of the advantage that will result from the Divine service of *teshuvah* (which is more powerful[65] [than ordinary Divine service]), [we ask G-d] to "act generously with us," and [consider it] as if at the outset, (at the

---

64. On this basis, we can appreciate the connection of this statement [with its authors], Rabbi Menachem [and Rabbi Avin]. The name Menachem (מנחם) shares the same root as the word *nechamah* (נחמה), which also has the connotation of regret, and thus is associated with *teshuvah*.

[A connection can also be made with] the name Avin based on the explanations in *Likkutei Sichos*, Vol. IV, p. 1080, with regard to the advantage of *Av*, "the father," over *Menachem*, i.e., that with regard to *Menachem*, the lack associated with hardship is felt. {And yet, just as one must bless [G-d] for good, one must also bless [Him] for bad" (*Berachos* 60b).} From the level of *Av*, in contrast, the good that the evil contains is revealed. Thus it is possible to say that the name of Rabbi Avin is cited to allude to the concept that, through *teshuvah* motivated by love, willful transgressions can be transformed into merits.

65. See *Zohar*, Vol. I, p. 129b.

time a person performed the sins), his intent was to bring about that ascent.[66]

XII. There is a connection between these three requests {— bring us from the life of this world to the life of the World to Come... sustain us according to our deeds... [and] although we have brought evil upon You, act generously with us" —} and Yosef. Indeed, because of this connection, Yosef's conduct is referred to as a paradigm of these qualities.

[To explain:] From an inner perspective, the difference between Yaakov and Yosef is[67] that Yaakov's spiritual level

---

66. See *Likkutei Sichos,* Vol. V, p. 66ff. [translated in this series] and notes which explain that the concept that "there is nothing else aside from Him" (*Devarim* 4:39) is not affected by sins although they are against His will. For on the contrary, even they reveal how "there is nothing else aside from Him."

{In addition to the fact that the *teshuvah* (which comes after the performance of a sin) reveals the infinite dimension of G-dliness, that even the sparks of holiness which are found in purposeful sins can be elevated and transformed into merits,} through the sins themselves it is revealed that "there is nothing else aside from Him."

This revelation comes, however, {not through the sins themselves, but rather} from the fact that they are of no consequence before Him and He is not concerned with them. [Trans. Note: Unlike other dimensions of Divine service which themselves express G-d's qualities, the cycle of sin and *teshuvah* does not express a positive attribute of G-dliness. It does, however, show that nothing — even something that is against His will — can prevent His expression. For despite the barriers sins cause, the sins will ultimately be nullified. This demonstrates that their existence — i.e., an existence apart from G-d — is of no genuine importance.]

Similar concepts apply with regard to the essence of the Jewish soul (which is united with G-d's essence). Sin reveals the power of [the soul's] connection to G-d, showing:

a) that despite having committed a sin, it can still turn to G-d in *teshuvah.* Indeed, ultimately, every Jew will do *teshuvah* (*Tanya,* the conclusion of ch. 39);

b) that even at the time of the sin itself, it remained faithful to Him. For the sin is of no consequence and cannot detract from the connection of the essence of the soul to G-d.

67. See *Biurei HaZohar LeAdmur HaEmtzaei,* p. 30a ff.; *Or HaTorah, Vayechi* 386a,b. {That source [also explains that Yosef's Divine service is expressed through the verse (*Bereishis* 30:25):] "May G-d grant me another son," i.e., that Yosef

(as he exists for himself) reflects the world of *Atzilus*, while Yosef's level involves bringing Yaakov's spiritual qualities into the worlds of *Beriah*, *Yetzirah*, and *Asiyah*, and even into this material world which is "filled with *kelipah* and *sitra achra*."[68] [Yosef's Divine service involves] making Yaakov's spiritual qualities — *Atzilus* [i.e., overt G-dliness] — appreciated even within these lower levels.

To explain this in terms of our own Divine service: The essence of the soul (the levels of *chayah* and *yechidah*) reflect the level of *Atzilus*. The dimensions of the soul which descend into the worlds of *Beriah*, *Yetzirah*, and *Asiyah* represent merely a ray of the soul, the levels of *nefesh*, *ruach*, and *neshamah*.

[On this basis, we can appreciate] the achievement of Yosef. He made it possible for the essence of the soul to be felt and to have an effect with [a person's] intellectual comprehension ([which parallels the level of] *neshamah*, equivalent to *Beriah*), in his emotional qualities of love and fear ([which parallel the level of] *ruach*, equivalent to *Yetzirah*) and even in actual deed ([which parallels the level of] *nefesh*, equivalent to *Asiyah*). Moreover, it will even come into expression in the fulfillment of *mitzvos* for self-interest that is motivated by the animal soul ([which parallels] our material world which is filled with *kelipah* and *sitra achra*).

This reflects the connection between Yosef and the three requests mentioned above. Yosef made it possible for the essence of the soul to be manifest in this material world as it is manifest in the higher realms.[69] This makes it possible for the satisfaction of the Creator, the influence from G-d's essence {for the essence of the soul is connected with

---

transforms another — the *sitra achra* and the animal soul which are others [— estranged from G-d —] into a "son."}

68. *Tanya*, ch. 36 (p. 45b); see also ch. 7 (p. 11b).
69. See *Biurei HaZohar*, *loc. cit.*, which states that [Yosef's Divine service causes the soul to be manifest in this material world] "without a change in its nature, as it exists in the higher realms."

G-d's essence}, to be manifest within our Divine service in this material realm. This in turn brings about [G-d's] bringing us "from the life of this world to the life of the World to Come."

Through Yosef drawing down the essence of the soul even into the world of *Asiyah,* the "satisfaction of the Creator" is drawn down into our observance of the *mitzvos,* even when they are performed without vitality, [as mentioned with regard to the request,] "Sustain us according to our deeds."

Through drawing down the essence of the soul even into this physical world which is filled with *kelipah* and *sitra achra,* G-d's essence is drawn down even in the merits which result from the transformation of purposeful sins, [as mentioned with regard to the request,] "although we have brought evil upon You, act generously with us."

XIII. On this basis, we can appreciate the inner meaning of Yosef sustaining his brothers as it applies in a spiritual context. Through Yosef sustaining his brothers[70] according to their deeds and treating them favorably although they did him harm, he blazed a path and empowered all Jews for all time. He granted them the potential to look at another Jew (not as he appears externally, but) rather as he exists from the standpoint of his essence, [that he is "an actual part of G-d"]. Therefore, he will reward him according to his deeds and "repay those who are culpable with goodness."

And through looking at another Jew with such an outlook, each person will arouse similar potentials within his own being, and the essence of his soul will shine in all of his matters. {This is why the trait of "repaying those who

---

70. See *ibid., loc. cit.,* which explains that the influence which Yosef drew down from *Atzilus* to *Beriah, Yetzirah,* and *Asiyah* represents the sustenance which Yosef gave to his brothers, [i.e., the spiritual level of the brothers was the world of *Beriah* and Yosef brought them nurture from *Atzilus*].

are culpable with goodness" is such a fundamental quality, and affects the essence of a Jew.}[71]

[Conduct of this kind} will lead to the fulfillment of our requests: to "bring us from the life of this world to the life of the World to Come... sustain us according to our deeds... [and] although we have brought evil upon You, act generously with us."

Adapted from *Sichos Shabbos Parshas Chukas-Balak, Yud-Beis Tammuz, 5719;* and others

---

71.   [Trans. Note: The impetus to "repay those who are culpable with goodness" is the awareness of the essential G-dliness that lies at the core of the other person's being and in a larger sense, within everything that transpires within the world. Since whatever happens is an expression of G-dliness, even if on the surface it looks unfavorable, it is ultimately positive, and deserves to be repaid with kindness. The ability to appreciate this is an essential quality of the Jewish people.]

*   This was the beginning of the eightieth year [after the birth] of the Rebbe Rayatz, at which time, [according to the custom of saying the chapter of *Tehillim* which corresponds to the year,] the recitation of ch. 80 was begun (see also *Likkutei Sichos*, Vol. V, p. 103, and notes). That chapter contains the verse: "He led Yosef like sheep." It must be emphasized that Yosef was the first name of the Previous Rebbe. See *Likkutei Sichos*, Vol. III, p. 835.

Parshas Vayechi

Likkutei Sichos, Vol. XV, p. 432ff.

I. This week's Torah reading relates that when Yosef presented his two sons, Ephraim and Menasheh, before Yaakov for him to bless them, Yaakov placed his right hand on Ephraim and his left hand on Menasheh. When Yosef saw this: "It displeased him.... He told his father: 'No, father, this one (Menasheh) is the firstborn. Place your right hand on his head.'

"Yaakov answered him: 'I know, my son, I know.... He will also become great, yet his younger brother will become greater than he....' And he placed Ephraim before Menasheh."[1]

Explanation is necessary: The reason a firstborn receives a greater blessing than other children is that he possesses an advantage over them and [he deserves] greater importance than they do.[2] If Ephraim's level surpassed that of Menasheh[3] ("His younger brother will become greater than he"), why was it ordained from Above that Menasheh would be the firstborn, and not Ephraim?

From [the fact that Menasheh was the firstborn,] we can conclude that although "his younger brother will become

---

1. *Bereishis* 48:13-20.
2. See *ibid.* 49:3: "Reuven, you are my firstborn... [endowed with] greater rank and greater strength," and the commentaries of our Sages to that verse.
3. [Indeed, Ephraim's level so surpassed that of Menasheh] that Yaakov was not able to bless Menasheh that he would be greater than Ephraim. For [a blessing is capable only of empowering a potential which exists to be manifest, and] in their source, Ephraim is higher than Menasheh (*Likkutei Torah, Devarim*, p. 19a, the second *maamar* entitled *Ko Sivorchu 5626, et al*).

greater than he," Menasheh possessed an advantage over Ephraim and, because of that advantage, he was Yosef's firstborn. It is only that Yaakov's blessing emphasized a quality in which Ephraim surpassed Menasheh. Therefore [in this context,] he "placed Ephraim before Menasheh."

II. There is another concept involved. As mentioned many times, it is not appropriate to say that *tzaddikim* — and surely not the Patriarchs or Yaakov's sons — commit mistakes. In particular, this applies with regard to matters that were recorded in the Torah, [the Torah] of truth. Certainly, such matters represent eternal[4] truth.[5] Since the word Torah (תורה) is related to the word *horaah* (הוראה), meaning "instruction,"[6] these matters serve as eternal lessons for every Jew in each generation.

From this, it can be understood that Yosef did not state: "This one is the firstborn. Place your right hand on his (Menasheh's) head," because he erred and did not realize that "his younger brother will become greater than he." Instead, it was because he maintained that the advantage Menasheh possessed {because he was "the firstborn" (as stated in section I)} outweighed the advantage possessed by Ephraim.

Thus both concepts — Yosef's impression that the advantage Menasheh possessed is higher, and Yaakov's approach, that Ephraim's level is higher — are true. From the standpoint of Yosef's attributes (and Divine service), Menasheh is higher,[7] while from the standpoint of Yaakov's attributes (and Divine service), Ephraim is higher.

---

4. To quote *Tanya*, ch. 17: "The Torah is eternal." See *Likkutei Sichos*, Vol. V, *Sichas Parshas Vayigash*, p. 240ff. [translated in this series].
5. A slight question may be raised based on *Bereishis* 31:32 and *Rashi's* commentary to that verse.
6. *Zohar*, Vol. III, p. 53b.
7. This explanation also clarifies why in Yaakov's blessing to Yosef (as interpreted by *Rashi*, see the *Maskil LeDavid*) *Bereishis* 48:15-16: "May the angel who has delivered me bless the youths...," Menasheh is mentioned before

Thus we see that with regard to Yosef's relationship with his two sons, Menasheh is the firstborn, and the power of his father is manifest in him more than in his other son.[8] With regard to their relationship to *Yaakov*, by contrast, the order is, "The two sons born to you... are *mine*.... *I* will consider Ephraim and Menasheh as Reuven and Shimon."[9] In this statement, Ephraim[10] is placed before Menasheh and is compared to Reuven, Yaakov's firstborn.[11]

III. The difference between Menasheh and Ephraim — and also the advantage each of them possesses and the reason Menasheh shares a closer connection to Yosef, and Ephraim to Yaakov's (blessing) — can be understood through [an analysis of] the differences between their names.

Menasheh (מנשה) was given his name, because "G-d made me forget (נשני) all my struggle and all my father's home."[12] And Ephraim (אפרים) was given his name, because "G-d has made me fruitful (הפרני) in the land of my oppression."[13] Both of these names express the feelings which the descent to Egypt evoked within Yosef, but each name communicates an opposite thrust.

The name Menasheh reminds Yosef that he "was made to forget... his father's house" — {i.e., he realizes that he is living in a place which makes him vault away[14] (and forget)

Ephraim, although this was after Yaakov "maneuvered his hands," [and placed his right hand on Ephraim's head] (*ibid.*:14).

8. See *Shaar HaMitzvos* (from the *AriZal*), *Parshas Yisro; Likkutei Torah* [of the *AriZal*] *Parshas Vayeira*.

9. *Bereishis* 48:5.

10. See also *Rashi's* commentary (*Bereishis* 48:1) which states that Ephraim would frequently study with Yaakov. Note also *Vayikra Rabbah* 2:3.

11. Note the commentary of the *Alshich* to this verse. See also the *Midrash HaGadol* and *Bereishis Rabbah* 6:4; *Pesikta Rabasi*, ch. 3.

12. *Bereishis* 41:51.

13. *Ibid.* 41:52.

14. The interpretation of the root נשה given by *Rashi* in *Bereishis* 32:33. This explains why *Rashi* (in contrast to the Ibn Ezra and the *Rashbam*) does not explain the derivation of the term. Similarly, he does not explain the meaning

his father's home}. This name expresses his great yearning[15] (not to forget, and on the contrary,) to remain connected with his father's home. The name Ephraim, by contrast, reflects praise and thanksgiving for "mak[ing] me fruitful in the land of my oppression, [focusing] on the advantage and positive attributes which accrued to [Yosef] in Egypt.

These two concepts reflect two [general] thrusts of the Jews' Divine service in "the land of their oppression," in exile:[16] One of the modes of Divine service puts the emphasis on not being affected by one's surrounding environment, by remaining in touch with one's "father's home" (the situation in which the person existed before his descent into exile). The person continually reminds himself that he is living in a situation that makes him forget his father's home. And [these efforts] prevent him from forgetting.[17]

The second mode emphasizes how the person's Divine service concerns "the land of my oppression" and [confronts] the darkness of exile. He is not (to the same degree) concerned with remembering "his father's home." Instead, he labors to (illuminate the darkness of the exile with the light of holiness. These efforts also elevate the person himself and create a positive advantage within his

---

of the term הפרני, for it can be understood from his commentary to *Bereishis* 26:22.

[Trans. Note: With this note, the Rebbe is alluding to his frequently repeated thesis that *Rashi* does not restate the definition of the meaning of a term unless questions in the meaning of the new verse require him to do so.]

15. On this basis, we can understand why [Yosef gave his son] a name that focuses on his forgetting everything about his father's home (as the *Alshich* asks in his commentary to this verse). [For the intent is not to celebrate the forgetting, but to use it as a prod to remember.]

16. Note the teachings of the *Noam Elimelech* to *Bereishis* 48:13.

17. [Trans. Note: The person on this level of Divine service is affected internally by the challenges of exile and he experiences a descent. Nevertheless, he labors to make sure that this descent does not affect his conduct. In doing so, he expresses the fundamental power his G-dly soul possesses, that even in a negative environment, it can still manifest its power (See *Likkutei Sichos*, Vol. V, p. 96ff., and Vol. XV, p. 144ff., where similar concepts are explained).]

personality.) And through these efforts, the person "becomes fruitful in the land of his oppression."[18]

IV. The reason why Ephraim's potential is considered higher than Menasheh's is that the ultimate purpose of the descent to Egypt (and in a larger sense, the descent into exile) is that it is a descent for the sake of ascent,[19] to reach a position above the level that preceded the descent. {This involves not only not forgetting one's father's home, but also (and primarily) making a change within [the environment of] the exile,} enabling it to attain a higher level through the descent, being "fruitful in the land of oppression."

Nevertheless, Menasheh is still the firstborn. For with regard to birth[20] (revelation), i.e., Divine service in a revealed, active sense, Menasheh must come before Ephraim. Before one can achieve within "the land of oppression," which is associated with the mode of "doing good,"[21] one must first ensure that one will not be affected by the darkness of exile — the mode of "turning away from evil"[20] — by continually remembering (and thus remaining in contact with) his father's home.

The ultimate intent, however, is the [subsequent] ascent, [the Divine service of] Ephraim. And therefore, Ephraim is mentioned first in Yaakov's blessing.[22] For in the

---

18. [Trans. Note: In this mode of Divine service, the person's attention is not focused on his own personal spiritual growth, but rather on his achievements within his environment. See the *sichos* mentioned in the previous note.]

19. Cf. *Makkos* 8a.

20. See *Rashi's* commentary to *Bereishis* 25:26 [which indicates that the ultimate purpose is not the first to be revealed].

21. Cf. *Tehillim* 34:15. Note the sources cited in note 11 which explain that Ephraim and Menasheh are parallel to Reuven and Shimon respectively. *Torah Or* (at the beginning of *Parshas Vayechi*), [it] explains that Reuven is identified with the attribute of *chesed* (kindness), while Shimon is identified with *gevurah* (might).

22. For at the source, he is the most elevated. See the sources mentioned in note 3.

blessing and endowment of power from Above for Divine service during the exile, Ephraim is more important. And therefore, "he placed Ephraim before Menasheh."[23]

V. A deeper explanation of the above: There are several dimensions to the advantage and the higher quality which a Jew achieves through his service in (the darkness of) exile:

a) The descent brings out the power of the soul, showing that it is not influenced by the darkness of exile, just as an opponent calls forth a person's attribute of victory.[24] In a similar vein, [the Baal Shem Tov interprets[25] the verse:[26] "My soul thirsts for You (because I am) in a parched land... so may I see You in the Sanctuary," [as a request that the desire for G-dliness felt when distant, continue after he comes close again].

b) A deeper purpose: The great descent expresses the deeper, inner power of the soul which is unbounded. This power enables the soul {not only to remain undiminished, for exile will cause it to descend, but on the contrary,} to influence his surroundings and elevate them to his level, transforming the darkness of the exile into light.[27]

---

23. This sequence must also be reflected within a person's individual Divine service. Although [chronologically,] when actually performing one's Divine service, the mode of Menasheh comes first (as above), in a person's preparation, primacy must be given to the mode of Ephraim. For before descending into exile, a person must appreciate that the descent is for the sake of ascent. Only with such [a mindset] will the first stages of Divine service ("turning away from evil," laboring not to forget "one's father's home") be able to be carried out appropriately.

24. See the *maamar* entitled *Tzidkas Pirzono* in *Toras Chayim* (p. 323a ff.); the series of *maamarim* entitled *Basi LeGani 5710*, ch. 11.

25. *Kesser Shem Tov*, Addendum, sec. 52, *et al.*

26. *Tehillim* 63:2.

27. [Trans. Note: The first advantage reflects how the soul is not affected by the darkness of exile. The second advantage demonstrates that not only can the soul withstand challenge, the soul can become a contributory influence, changing its surroundings for the better. The ability to make such a change indicates that the soul's power is unlimited; it is not confined to a particular setting and can bring out positive energy in any situation.]

These two qualities, however, reflect the advantages and positive qualities which the soul brings out [based on its own potential]. Exile [is merely a catalyst, enabling] this advantage (which the soul possesses in potential) to be expressed through Divine service]. There is, nevertheless, a higher positive quality which the soul expresses (through its Divine service in exile) [that makes exile a positive influence]:

c) Through transforming the darkness of exile to light, the soul receives a positive quality which it does not possess within its own potential. To cite a parallel: a *baal teshuvah* who possesses merits that come from the transformation of sins, [a positive quality] which a *tzaddik* does not possess.[28]

VI. On this basis, we can appreciate the difference between Menasheh and Ephraim. Both brothers are Yosef's children, i.e., they both reveal his personal quality [which was expressed in the verse explaining his name]:[29] "May G-d add to me another son." [Yosef's Divine service] involves an increase which is brought about through Divine service in exile (making from the *sitra achra*, "the other," a son[30]). But this service involves two levels:[31]

Menasheh — the powerful memory of one's father's home — the power of the soul which is revealed within Yosef through his Divine service in Egypt.

---

28. A parallel also exists within the Divine service of every person: the yearning, and the love of G-d "with all your might" that is generated within the G-dly soul through [the influence] of the animal soul (see *Torah Or*, p. 39c-d; see also *Sefer HoArachim Chabad*, erech *Ahavas HaShem*, sec. "the advantage contributed by the animal soul," which discusses this matter at length.)

29. *Bereishis* 30:24.

30. *Or HaTorah, Vayeitze*, p. 220a ff.; *Vayechi*, p. 386a,b, *et al.*

31. See the series of *maamarim* entitled *Yom Tov Shel Rosh HaShanah 5666* (p. 384), which explains that Yosef contains two dimensions: how he exists in connection with Yaakov, and how he exists when separated from him, in which instance, Yosef was more successful.

Ephraim — the higher quality of light which is drawn down from the darkness itself. "G-d made me fruitful in the land of my oppression."

Since the higher level is reached through the positive quality which is drawn down from the transformation of darkness; therefore, Ephraim is placed before Menasheh.

VII. Based on the above, it is difficult to understand the connection of Menasheh to Yosef and of Ephraim to Yaakov. For on the surface, the opposite appears to be true. Menasheh, who brings to mind "my father's home," seems to have a greater connection with Yaakov, while Ephraim, being "fruitful in the land of my oppression," appears to share a more direct connection with Yosef, the increase which comes about through the Divine service of "May G-d add to me another son."[32]

This question can be resolved through the explanation of the verse:[9] "And now the two sons born to you in the land of Egypt before I came to you in Egypt are mine. I will consider Ephraim and Menasheh as Reuven and Shimon." There is a difficulty in this verse.[33] On the surface, it would have been sufficient to say: "And now your two sons Ephraim and Menasheh are mine. I will consider Ephraim and Menasheh as Reuven and Shimon." Why is it necessary for the verse to add the phrase "born to you in the land of Egypt before I came to you in Egypt"?

It is possible to explain that the verse is doing more than mentioning which of Yosef's sons will be counted in the reckoning of the tribes. It is also giving a rationale and explanation as to why they are connected to Yaakov ("they are mine"). "They are mine" because they were born to Yosef "in the land of Egypt," and moreover, they were born "before I came to you in Egypt." The intent is that although

---

32. See *Or HaTorah, Yirmeyahu,* pp. 378-381.
33. See the commentary of the *Alshich* and others on the verse, and the commentary of the *Ramban* to *Bereishis* 48:15.

they were born in Egypt and raised in an environment distant from Yaakov, they nevertheless conducted themselves as Yaakov's grandchildren. This demonstrates that "They are mine"; they express Yaakov's true perfection.[34]

VIII. Based on the above, we can explain why Yaakov mentioned Ephraim before Menasheh in this context (as stated above, section II): Since Menasheh reflects how the memory and the connection to "my father's home" has not [entirely] ceased (as explained above at great length), this mode of service does not truly reflect how [Yosef existed] "before I came to you in Egypt." For there is constantly (a memory of) "my father's home."

It is, in contrast, the Divine service of Ephraim which truly reflects the situation "before I came to you in Egypt." In this mode of service, the person lives in "the land of my oppression," and (on the surface) the connection with Yaakov ("my father's home") is not obvious. Nevertheless, he carries out his Divine service in a manner that reveals how he is Yaakov's grandchild.

IX. In *Chassidus*[35] it is explained that Yaakov is identified with "the attribute of truth which extends from one end to the other,"[36] from the highest extreme to the lowest extreme. This motif is manifest through Yosef. For the level of Yaakov (as he exists for himself) is *Atzilus,* above the realms of *Beriah, Yetzirah,* and *Asiyah.* It is Yosef who brings Yaakov's level (*Atzilus*) into these lower realms, and in particular into this material world (the lowest extreme).

---

34. For it is with regard to Yaakov that it is said: "His bed is perfect." (*Vayikra Rabbah* 36:5, *Rashi's* commentary, *Bereishis* 48:31; see also *Pesachim* 56a, and other sources.)

35. *Biurei HaZohar* (of the Mitteler Rebbe), p. 29c; and from the *Tzemach Tzedek,* p. 168ff; *Or HaTorah, Vayechi,* the *maamar* entitled *Ben Poras,* and its explanation (p. 385b ff.; Vol. VI, p. 1147b ff.; Vol. V, p. 993b ff., Vol. VI, p. 1122b ff.).

36. *Zohar,* Vol. II, p. 175b; *Tanya,* the conclusion of ch. 13.

{This is the inner motivating factor as to why Yaakov's descent to Egypt came about because of Yosef. [Egypt (*Mitzrayim*) is identified with *meitzarim* ("boundaries" and "limitations"). Yosef draws Yaakov down into] the boundaries and limitations of the worlds of *Beriah, Yetzirah,* and *Asiyah.*}

Similar concepts apply with regard to the other extreme: Through the transformation of darkness (the worlds of *Beriah, Yetzirah,* and *Asiyah*) into light — transforming an "other" into a "son" — the higher quality of light is brought out from the darkness, attaining a level above *Atzilus* (Yaakov's own spiritual level).[37]

This also explains[38] why the seventeen years that Yaakov spent in Egypt were his best years, as implied by the verse:[39] "And Yaakov lived in the land of Egypt seventeen years." For through the descent into Egypt, he achieved his personal fulfillment. [He demonstrated how his virtue could be expressed in all situations,] extending from the highest extreme to the lowest extreme.

X. Since Ephraim and Menasheh replace Yosef in the reckoning of the tribes, it can be concluded that they reflect "the posterity of Yaakov, Yosef."[40] They manifest Yaakov's qualities in the land of Egypt. And in doing so, they contribute a dimension over and above that of Yosef.

When Yosef descends into Egypt (in the analogue, the worlds of *Beriah, Yetzirah,* and *Asiyah*), *Atzilus,* Yaakov's level, is revealed overtly. Since through [Yosef's] Divine

---

37. See the *maamar* entitled *Ben Poras* cited above; see also *Or HaTorah, loc. cit.,* p. 354a; Vol. VI. p. 1123a.
38. See *Biurei HaZohar, loc. cit., Or HaTorah,* Vols. V and VI, *loc. cit.*
39. *Bereishis* 47:28. See the commentary of the *Baal HaTurim* and others to this verse. Note the teaching of the Alter Rebbe explaining their statements (*HaYom Yom,* p. 12, clarified at length in *Likkutei Sichos,* Vol. X, p. 160ff.). See also *Zohar,* Vol. I, p. 216b.
40. *Bereishis* 37b. See the sources cited in note 35. See also the passage from *Or HaTorah, Yirmeyahu,* cited in note 32, sec. 1, with regard to Ephraim.

service, Yaakov's influence which is above Egypt (i.e., *Beriah, Yetzirah,* and *Asiyah*),[41] shines openly, Egypt does not bring about concealment. On the contrary, Yosef becomes the ruler of Egypt.

Thus Yosef's Divine service does not involve a genuine descent (and involvement with) the darkness of Egypt (the lowest extreme). [For due to Yosef's influence,] the darkness [does not] oppose the light of holiness.

{This is reflected in the events which actually transpired. As long as Yosef was alive, there were no harsh decrees against the Jewish people. It was as if the Jews had not descended into Egypt. It was only when Yosef died that the descent became distinct; "On that day, it was as if [the Jews] entered Egypt."[42]}

It is through [Ephraim and Menasheh], "the two sons born to you in the land of Egypt before I came to you in Egypt," i.e., Divine service in a place where Yaakov's influence is not openly visible, a level where the darkness of Egypt can conceal and oppose holiness, that Yaakov's quality achieves consummate expression, [for their Divine service demonstrates how his virtue is expressed in all situations,] extending from the highest extreme to the lowest extreme.[43]

XI. The three levels described above:

41. See the sources in *Biurei HaZohar* and *Or HaTorah* cited above which explain that the task of refinement achieved by Yosef involves "elevating [dimensions] of *Beriah* to *Atzilus,* until they are actually on the level of *Atzilus.*"

42. *Shmos Rabbah* 1:4; *Midrash Tanchuma, Shmos,* sec. 3. See the explanation of this at length in *Likkutei Sichos,* Vol. VI, p. 31ff.

43. See a similar concept explained in *Likkutei Sichos,* Vol. X, (p. 164, note 32), clarifying the advantage of the Divine service of Yaakov's other sons {whose spiritual level is in the realms of *Beriah, Yetzirah,* and *Asiyah;* their Divine service involves the refinement of the world of separation, (see the sources mentioned in note 40} over Yosef.

See also *Pelach HaRimon, Parshas Vayechi,* (p. 121a) which explains that the fact that Yaakov's sons illuminate the realm of *Beriah* is because their source is the level of Yaakov whose potential is to extend from the highest extreme to the lowest extreme.

a) the level of Yaakov, who is higher than Egypt by
virtue of his own [spiritual level],

   b) Yosef, who illuminates Egypt because of the influence of Yaakov, and

   c) Yosef's sons who relate to the darkness of Egypt, as it
exists within its own frame of reference,
reflect the three positive qualities (enumerated in sec. V)
that are expressed through the descent into exile.

   The first quality — that because of the spiritual power
of the soul, the exile cannot bring about a descent for the
soul (but the darkness of exile itself is not transformed)
[— reflects distance]. It is as if the two are separate,[44] [for
one is] above the exile {like Yaakov,[45] whose own level was
too high to descend to [the mindset of] Egypt.}[46]

---

44. [Trans. Note: The two are not separate, for the person is actually living in
     exile, but his spiritual level and Divine service are above the exile and he is
     not concerned with the exile at all, e.g., a person who lives in a cloistered
     Torah community without contact with the outside world.]

45. See *Or HaTorah*, the explanation to the *maamar* entitled *Ben Poras* (p. 388b ff.,
     Vol. VI, 1147b ff.) which identifies Yaakov with the first revelations of the
     kav, [the vector of Divine light that shines after the initial *tzimtzum*,] which is
     above the [task of] refinement carried out in *Beriah*, *Yetzirah*, and *Asiyah*. (See
     also *ibid.*, p. 1148a.)

46. Therefore even as Yaakov descended to Egypt, he remained above the dark-
     ness of Egypt. There was, however, an advantage achieved through his
     descent into Egypt above his previous level. For even in a place of darkness,
     the light retained its power. This reflects the higher quality of light (that it
     has the potential to shine even in a place of darkness). See *Likkutei Sichos*,
     Vol. X, p. 163.

     [Trans. Note: The above mentioned *sichah* explains that there are two
     interpretations of the phrase (*Koheles* 2:13): "the advantage of light over
     darkness." The first interpretation is straightforward. When light shines into
     darkness, the advantage that light possesses over darkness is revealed. (For
     the darkness retreats before the light.)

     The second interpretation understands the word יתרון translated as "advan-
     tage," as meaning "higher quality." The higher quality of light comes about
     from the transformation of darkness.

     Developing these concepts further, the three levels described in our *sichah*
     can be explained as follows: The Divine service of Yaakov described here
     reflects the motif of *gilui milimaaleh limatah*: a revelation from above. In this
     motif, although the lower realms are illuminated, the illumination is not
     internalized. To cite an analogy, when a window is opened and a dark room

The second quality expresses the strength of the soul, [that it is so powerful that] nothing can oppose it, and thus even the darkness of exile will be transformed into light. This parallels the level of Yosef[47] who draws down the level of Yaakov into Egypt. And thus the transformation of darkness to light comes about because of the revelation of *Atzilus* (Yaakov)[48] in *Beriah, Yetzirah,* and *Asiyah* (Egypt).

---

is illuminated, the nature of the room has not changed. Although now it is brightly lit, that light is a function of the sun shining from the outside and not of the room itself. Similarly, in the analogue, although Yaakov lived in Egypt and revealed G-dly light there, that light was not internalized within that foreign land.

The levels of Yosef and his sons reflect the service of *haalah milimatah limaalah,* ascent upward. The lower rung is elevated and lifted to a higher level. The classic example used to illustrate this mode is a student who studies and elevates his understanding. Once he has learned new concepts, he has changed himself; he now possesses a more developed intellectual potential than he did previously.

Within this level, there are two approaches: one student whose skills focus on his ability to recall his teacher's instruction. Since he has assimilated and internalized the wisdom he was taught, his own level has advanced. Nevertheless, his advance is due primarily to the influence received from his teacher. He has not changed his own thinking processes fundamentally.

The second approach is illustrated by a student who was taught, not only to parrot his teacher, but to deal with new and different conceptual frameworks according to the mindset of his teacher. See *Likkutei Sichos,* Vol. X, p. 82, which explains similar concepts while interpreting *Avos* 2:9 which describes R. Eliezer ben Horkenus as "a cemented cistern which does not lose a drop," i.e., he preserves his teacher's wisdom, and R. Elazar ben Arach: "as a stream that flows with ever-increasing strength," i.e., he extends his teacher's wisdom to new and different situations concerning which he had not received instruction from him.

Similarly, Yosef's Divine service reflected the thrust of *haalah* (ascent), but as the *sichah* explains, his contributions come as a result of Yaakov's influence, like the student whose skill is in recalling his teacher's instruction. The Divine service of Menasheh and (more so) of Ephraim parallels the achievements of a student who is able to take his teacher's instruction to new frontiers.]

47. See the *maamarim* from *Or HaTorah* cited in note 44, which explain that Yosef is the final point of the *kav* which brings about refinement in the realms of *Beriah, Yetzirah,* and *Asiyah* (as reflected in the interpretation of the verse "May G-d add to me another son").

48. This reflects the difference between the transformation of darkness into light brought about because of the light, and the transformation of the darkness

[The third level reflects how] the higher quality of light which is drawn down by the darkness itself is achieved (fundamentally[49]) through the service in the darkness of Egypt when Yaakov's influence is not apparent.[46] [This Divine service is performed by those] "born to you in the land of Egypt before I came to you."

XII. Based on the above, we can appreciate the connection between Menasheh and Yosef (which caused him to be Yosef's firstborn), and the bond Ephraim shares with Yaakov.[50] The Divine service of Menasheh focuses on revealing the remembrance of "my father's home" (and through this to transform the darkness of Egypt). This resembles[51] the Divine service of Yosef that draws down (into revelation) the influence of Yaakov into *Beriah, Yetzirah,* and *Asiyah,* and through this, brings about transformation.

The consummate expression of Yaakov's [spiritual potential] comes when the higher quality of light is revealed from the darkness itself. This is accomplished by Ephraim,[52]

---

itself. (See the series of *maamarim* entitled *BeShaah SheHikdimu 5672,* Vol. III, p. 1325ff. and *Likkutei Sichos,* Vol. IX, p. 63.)

49. Even when the darkness is transformed because of the light, a higher quality of light is brought out because of the darkness. Nevertheless, the true concept of this advantage (stemming from the ultimate source of the darkness) comes about when the darkness is transformed on its own initiative, as explained in the series of *maamarim* entitled *BeShaah SheHikdimu 5672, loc. cit.* (which explains that the attributes of *gevurah* can be sweetened only in their source).

50. See the passage from the *Noam Elimelech* cited in note 15 above.

51. [Although Menasheh's Divine service resembles Yosef's,] it is not entirely the same. For Yaakov's spiritual qualities shone openly for Yosef, while Menasheh possesses only a remembrance of "his father's house." (For as reflected in the actual events, [Menasheh] was born "before [Yaakov] came to... Egypt.")

52. Some explanation is necessary regarding the above (and the statements in sec. VIII, note 42), for the passage from *Or HaTorah, Yirmeyahu* cited in note 31 (sec. 1, 8), states that Ephraim's spiritual level is in *Atzilus.* Like Yosef's, it is above that of Yaakov's other sons.

[for his Divine service reflects how]: "G-d made me fruitful in the land of my oppression."

XIII. The Jewish people as a collective are referred to with the name Yosef, as it is written:[53] "He leads Yosef like sheep." From this, we can appreciate that every Jew must express himself in both thrusts of Divine service: that of Menasheh and that of Ephraim.[54]

First, he must begin with the wish and the yearning to be in "his father's home," to be in an environment which transcends exile. His descent into a world where G-dliness is concealed (in order to refine the exile) must be "compelled by [G-d's] decree."[55] Consequently, as soon as he completes his mission in the place of exile to which Divine Providence directed him, he hurries back to a place where he can devote himself entirely to matters of holiness, Torah, and Divine service.[56]

Nevertheless, throughout the time a person is involved in his or her mission in exile, he cannot remain content with the Divine service of Menasheh. He cannot satisfy himself with the knowledge that he has not forgotten his father's home and has not been influenced by his environment.

This alone [is not sufficient]. His Divine service must serve as a preparation for the consummation of the ultimate intent: "that G-d make me fruitful in the land of my oppres-

---

53. *Tehillim* 80:2; see the commentaries of *Rashi* and *Metzudos David* to the verse.

54. As reflected in the blessing that Yaakov gave [Ephraim and Menasheh] (*Bereishis* 48:20): "Through you, Israel [— every single member of our people —] shall be blessed.... May G-d make you as Ephraim and Menasheh."

55. Cf. the Pesach *Haggadah*; see also *Shabbos* 89b. [See also *Likkutei Sichos*, Vol. IV, p. 1219.]
   This does not conflict with the concept stated further in the text that the Divine service of Ephraim must be carried out with happiness. See *Sichas Lag BaOmer*, 5738.

56. This directive can be derived from Mordechai's act in leaving Persia — where he served as second to the king — and ascended to *Eretz Yisrael* (*Sichas Motzo'ei Shabbos Shemini*, 5738).

sion,"[57] illuminating the darkness of exile with "the lamp of *mitzvah* and the light of Torah,"[58] until that darkness is transformed into light: [and] "The night will shine as the day."[59]

(Adapted from *Sichos Shabbos Parshas Vayechi*, 5730)

---

57. It is noteworthy that the entire Jewish people are referred to as Ephraim (*Yirmeyahu* 31:19, *et al.*), but not as Menasheh (*Ramban*, commentary to *Bereishis* 48:16).
58. Cf. *Mishlei* 6:23.
59. *Tehillim* 139:12. The intent is that the darkness will shine on its own (see *Sefer HaArachim Chabad, Erech or biyachas lichoshech, et al.*; see also the series of *maamarim* entitled *BeShaah SheHikdimu 5672*, Vol. III, p. 1346.

Parshas Shmos

Likkutei Sichos, Vol. VI, p. 13ff.

I. The *Talmud* explains[1] that the verse:[2] "And they embittered their lives with mortar and bricks, and all [sorts of] work in the field, all their work...," [reflects a sequence]. First, they compelled them to work with "mortar and bricks." Afterwards, they were forced to do "all [sorts of] work in the field," and ultimately,[3] "all their work."

The commentaries[4] explain the *Talmud's* intent as follows: One might ask: Why does the verse single out "mortar and bricks"? Seemingly, these tasks are also included in "all their work." Therefore the *Talmud* explains that "mortar and bricks" came first. It was the beginning of their "work in the field." Therefore the verse mentions it (first and) as a separate category.

Every concept in the Torah is extremely precise. The fact that the work with "mortar and bricks" came first (and only afterwards came "all their work") reflects more than chronological precedence. It was also the most significant and most difficult element of their enslavement. When describing the enslavement of the Jews in Egypt with a general statement, one would say that they performed work with "mortal and bricks." Afterwards, as one begins to explain the various particulars, one would speak of their "work in the field."

---

1. *Sotah* 11b.
2. *Shmos* 1:14.
3. See *Shmos Rabbah* 1:11; see all the *Chidushei Aggados* of the *Maharsha* to *Sotah*, *loc. cit.*, who interprets the *Talmudic* passage in this manner.
4. See the *Chidushei Aggados, loc. cit.*

From this, we can conclude that even ultimately, when the Jews performed "all their work," the core of their enslavement involved making bricks.[5] This concept is also reflected in the ensuing phases of the narrative, for when Pharaoh desired to "make the work difficult for the men,"[6] {— an event which took place in the final phases of the enslavement in Egypt, after Moshe and Aharon had already come to Pharaoh as G-d's emissaries and told him to release the people —} he sought to accomplish this, (not through any other type of work, but) through the task of making bricks. [He told his overseers] not to give the Jews any straw for the bricks, and yet to require them to produce the same quantity of bricks in the same given amount of time as they had previously.

Moreover, throughout the time of the enslavement, the Jews' workday was primarily devoted to making bricks (although they also performed other tasks). This is understood from the interpretation the *Midrash* offers[7] to the verse:[8] "And the Egyptians made the children of Israel perform excruciating (בפרך) labor," as בפה רך, "with a soft tongue,"[9] [i.e., with deception]. Pharaoh himself took a basket and a rake and made bricks, and while performing this work, he told the Jewish people: "Work together with me today as a favor," i.e., that they should follow his example and make bricks.[10] [The Jews fell for his ploy, and] worked with him "with all their strength." When night fell, Pharaoh had a reckoning made of the bricks and told the Jews: "Prepare this amount every day."

---

5.   As *Rashi* states in his commentary to *Shmos* 24:10: "The Jews were enslaved in making bricks."
6.   *Shmos* 5a.
7.   *Bamidbar Rabbah* 15:20; *Midrash Tanchuma, Parshas Bahaaloscha*, sec. 13; *Tanchuma*, Buber edition, sec. 23; see also *Shmos Rabbah*, ch. 1.
8.   *Shmos* 1:13.
9.   See also *Sotah* 11b.
10.   See *ibid.* 11a.

Since every day, they had to prepare the same number of bricks that they had made on that first day when they had worked "with all their strength" for the entire day, it follows that throughout the later time of their enslavement, the overwhelming majority of their time — indeed, it could almost be said their entire time[11] — was spent making bricks.[12] The other work which they performed was carried out during the few extra hours they had and at night.[13]

On this basis, we can appreciate why the Torah mentions explicitly the Jews' work "with bricks and mortar." For even after they were compelled to perform "all their work," their primary occupation was making bricks.

---

11. We cannot say that they spent the entire day making bricks. For during a portion of the day, they built the cities for Pharaoh.* [It can, however, be said that building the cities] is also included in the work "with mortar and bricks." (See the *Maharsha*, loc. cit., who states that "in the beginning, they built cities for him." [In that vein, the phrase "with mortar and bricks"] can be interpreted "with mortar" — to make bricks — and "with bricks" — to build cities from them.

    The *Ramban* (in his commentary to *Shmos* 1:11) and the *Or HaChayim* (in his commentary to *Shmos* 1:14) state that building the cities is not included in the work "with bricks and mortar." They explain that, at the outset, the Jews began building cities, and only afterwards, were they forced to make bricks. [Despite their interpretation,] the simple meaning of the *Talmudic* and *Midrashic* passages indicates that [brick-making was their first and primary task], as explained above. See the *Or HaChayim* (in his commentary to *Shmos* 1:11) who states "According to their interpretation, one must say that words [of deception] (בפה רך) preceded the imposition of taskmasters."

    ---

    * It cannot be said that the Jews built the cities after nightfall, because:
      a) *Midrash Tanchuma, Parshas Vayeitzei*, sec. 9, states that "the work in the field" was performed "after they returned to their homes in the evening."
      b) According to this, building the cities ("one of the primary tasks performed by the Jewish people") is not at all mentioned in the verse "And they embittered their lives" (it is merely included as a secondary factor in "all their work").

12. See *Shmos Rabbah* 1:12 [which states that the Egyptians told the Jews]: "If you go to sleep in your homes... you will not complete your quota."

13. *Bereishis Rabbah* 27:2; *Midrash Tanchuma, Parshas Vayeitzei*, sec. 9.

II. To explain why the fundamental aspect of the Jews' enslavement[14] involved "mortar and bricks": As stated on a
different occasion at length,[15] the explanation of the verse:
"And Egypt enslaved the children of Israel... and they
embittered their lives" [refers to the Jews' spiritual vitality].
For the true vitality and the true energy of the Jewish people stems from holiness[16] (from their G-dly soul).[17]

The Egyptians desired [to subjugate this potential and]
use it to build storage cities for Pharaoh. Instead of the Jews
building a dwelling for G-d, building "the city of our G-d,"[18]
they were compelled by those "who cause them aggravation
and distress"[19] to use their holy powers to establish a
dwelling for kelipah, "storage cities for Pharaoh."

"One corresponds to the other."[20] "The city of our G-d"
is built from stone (just as a city is built from many houses,
and the houses built from stone[21] — for the fundamental
strength of a house depends on the stones with which it is
built).[22] The cities of kelipah, by contrast (for kelipah copies

---

14. This refers to the enslavement of the Jewish people in Egypt in an actual
    physical sense, and the spiritual exile and exodus from Egypt which every
    person must undergo, for "Each and every day, a person is obligated to see
    himself as if he left Egypt today" (Tanya, ch. 47, note the explanation there).
15. See Likkutei Sichos, Vol. II, p. 848ff.
16. For with regard to the Torah and its mitzvos, it is said (daily liturgy, evening
    service): "For they are our lives." See Kuntres U'Mayon, Discourse 7. See also
    the maamar entitled BeShaah SheHikdimu in the series of maamarim of that
    name from the year 5672 (ch. 2), which states: "For this reason, the type of
    activities in which a person is involved is very significant. For in each and
    every activity which a person performs, he introduces G-dly power." See also
    Likkutei Sichos, Vol. III, p. 848, note 22.
17. See Tanya, chs. 9 and 12, et al.
18. Cf. Tehillim 48:2. Note the interpretation in the notes of the Tzemach Tzedek to
    the verse.
19. Bereishis Rabbah 16:4 states that all the gentile powers who cause the Jews
    aggravation (מצירים) are called Egypt (מצרים).
20. ["The realm of unholiness corresponds to the realm of holiness" (Zohar, Vol.
    III, p. 47b, interpreting Koheles 7:14).]
21. See secs. 2 and 3 of the maamar entitled VeHayah HaNishar BiTziyon 5691, and
    sec. 3 of the maamar entitled Or LiArba Asor 5700, et al.
22. See Sefer HaYetzirah (the conclusion of ch. 4) which states: "Two stones build
    two houses...." Note also Negaim 12:2.

holiness as a monkey mimics man[23]) [are built from bricks].
And thus the essential enslavement of the Jewish people
involved making bricks (for "they used bricks in place of
stones"[24]), the building blocks for the Egyptian cities.

On this basis, we can understand why "mortar and
bricks" is mentioned before the general term "all of their
work" (as mentioned in sec. I). For the inner meaning of
every act that a person performs is building. When he performs a positive act, whether a *mitzvah* or an activity which
is neither commanded or forbidden, but is carried out "for
the sake of heaven"[25] or [in a manner which fulfills the
charge:[26]] "Know Him in all your ways," he adds a stone to
the building of holiness. And when he performs an undesirable act, he adds a brick to the building of *kelipah*. The
different nature of the activities is expressed in the type of
building, but there is a common factor shared by all the activities, they are all building. (Positive activities are building
Jerusalem, while negative activities are building Tyre.)[27]

III. Within stones themselves, there are two categories:
stones and bricks. Stones are created by G-d, while bricks
are fashioned by man.[28] The work performed by the Jews in
Egypt centered primarily (not on using stones, but) on
making bricks.

For this reason the *Beis HaMikdash*, the consummate expression of "the
city of our G-d," Jerusalem, was built primarily of stone, as will be explained
in secs. 5 and 8.

23. *Zohar*, Vol. II, p. 148b; *Yahel Or*, p. 358, which quotes our Sages' comment
(*Midrash HaGadol*), to *Bereishis* 5:3, [that between giving birth to Cain and
Hevel and giving birth to Shes,] Adam fathered monkey-like creatures.

24. Cf. *Bereishis* 11:3. See *Shaar HaPesukim*, the beginning of *Parshas Shmos*, and
Likkutei Torah, LiGimmel Parshiyos on the verse.

25. *Avos* 2:12.

26. *Mishlei* 3:6. See *Likkutei Sichos*, Vol. III, pp. 907, 932.

27. See *Rashi, Bereishis* 25:23, based on *Megillah* 6a, and see also *Zohar*, Vol. II, pp.
236a, 240a, [which explain that building Jerusalem leads to the destruction of
Tyre (Caesaria, according to some commentaries), and conversely, building
Tyre leads ו"נ to the destruction of Jerusalem].

28. See *Torah Or*, p. 77c; *Likkutei Torah, LiGimmel Parshiyos*, p. 72c ff.; See also the
maamar entitled *VeHayah HaNishar* cited above, sec. VII.

What is the difference between stones and bricks? Stones are created by G-d and allude to a high level of holiness.[29] Therefore, at the outset, the *Beis HaMikdash* was to be built from stone,[30] and *Eretz Yisrael* is praised[31] as "a land whose stones are iron."

Bricks, by contrast, refer to activities which are *reshus*, neither commanded nor forbidden,[32] but whose outcome — whether holiness or the opposite — depends on man's intention.

{For this reason, we find that the prohibition against prostrating oneself with outstretched hands and legs applies only on a stone floor, and not on a brick floor.[33] For the prohibition was instituted so that an activity — prostration — which resembles an activity performed in the *Beis HaMikdash*[34] should not be performed outside of the *Beis HaMikdash*. Since bricks do not allude to any element of holiness, prostrating oneself on a brick floor does not resemble the service of prostration performed in the *Beis HaMikdash*.}

---

29. See the *maamar* entitled *VeHayah HaNishar; Likkutei Torah, LiGimmel Parshiyos,* and *Torah Or, loc. cit.,*
30. *Rambam, Mishneh Torah, Hilchos Beis HaBechirah* 1:8.
31. *Devarim* 8:9.
32. See *Torah Or, loc. cit.*
33. *Magen Avraham, Orach Chayim* 131:20.
34. *Rashi, Megillah* 22b, entry *lo osra.* The *Rambam, Mishneh Torah, Hilchos Avodas Kochavim* 6:6ff (note the gloss of the *Kessef Mishneh*), in contrast, explains that the prohibition was instituted because it was a pagan practice. Even according to this interpretation, it is possible to explain that the pagans adopted this method of worship because it was one of the services in the *Beis HaMikdash.*

    {[To cite a parallel: The prohibition of sacrificing on] a monument (which is mentioned before the prohibition of prostrating oneself on a stone floor in the *Rambam*) was "cherished by the Patriarchs" (*Sifri, Devarim* 16:22), [but was forbidden afterwards because it was adopted by the pagans]. It is possible to explain that because it was cherished by the Patriarchs, it was adopted by the pagans (see *Rashi, Devarim, loc. cit.;* note also *Or HaTorah, Vayeitzei,* p. 198ff.).

    It must, however, be noted that the *Beis HaMikdash* (where there was a stone floor) was built many years after the commandment against prostrating oneself on a stone floor was given.

Indeed, bricks have (the potential [to be used] for) the opposite of holiness.[35] Thus the *Talmud*, when speaking about designating a false divinity,[36] gives as an example:[37] "He erected a brick."[38] A similar concept is reflected in *Rashi's* commentary[39] [explaining why the Tower of Bavel was built with bricks]: "For there are no stones in Bavel, for it is a valley." Since Bavel (and any valley[40]) is a low place, a place where the Divine light is concealed, a place of darkness, to the extent that the Torah applies the phrase:[41] "He set me down in a dark place," to the *Babylonian Talmud*.[42] Therefore the level of stones which are created by Heaven is not relevant to Bavel.

IV. Based on the above, it is possible to explain why the arduous labor the Jews had to perform in Egypt concerned

---

35. See *Pardes Shaar Erchi HaKinnuim, erech leveinah*; (quoted in *Or HaTorah, Shmos*, p. 24, the *maamar* entitled *Zos Chanukas 5640*, the conclusion of ch. 14; see also the *maamar* entitled *VeHayah HaNishar*, sec. 17) which states that "A brick is from the side of impurity."

36. [In a larger sense, this relates to all transgression, for when a person commits] even a minor transgression of a Rabbinic command, he becomes separate from the oneness and unity [of G-d], just as through the actual worship of false divinities. (see *Tanya*, chs. 24-25).

37. See *Avodah Zarah* 46a (see also *Sotah* 47a, although in some printings it was eliminated by the censor [which states that one of Yehoshua ben Parchia's students, presumably Yeshu of Nazareth, erected a brick and bowed down to it]).
      Note also [the interpretation of] *Eichah* 3:38: "From the mouth of the Most High will not issue forth evil."

38. See *Likkutei Torah, LiGimmel Parshiyos, loc. cit.*

39. To *Bereishis* 11:3.

40. Note *Sisrei Torah* to the *Zohar*, Vol. I, p. 75a, and our Sages' statement (*Eruvin* 6a): "He found a *bika*, and established a fence," [which interprets *bika*, the term interpreted here as valley, as open place"]. See also the *maamar* entitled *VeHayah HaNishar*, sec. 17, which interprets *bika* as referring to a place where there has been a rupture and there is separation.

41. *Eichah* 3:6.

42. [In its original, the *sichah* quotes the citation] as it appears in many sources within the *maamarim* of the Rebbeim. The concept is cited with this same wording in the *Shaloh, Beis Chochmah* (p. 16b) and *Beis HaGadol* (p. 36a). *Sanhedrin* 24a (quoted in the *Shaloh, Shaar HaGadol* (p. 35b) communicates the same concept using slightly different wording.

bricks and not stones. Since the purpose of their work was to build "storage cities for Pharaoh," the very opposite of "the city of our G-d," the building could not be performed with stones which reflect the realm of holiness, but rather with bricks, which are appropriate for "cities for Pharaoh."

This explanation is, however, insufficient. For, as explained above, the intent of the Egyptians was to use the power and vitality of holiness the Jews possessed to build the cities of *kelipah,* as indicated by the verse: "And Egypt enslaved the *children of Israel*... and they embittered *their lives.*"[43] Thus it would seem appropriate that they would have sought (and indeed, with greater intensity[44]) to use stones for their cities, for this would have enabled them to derive nurture from the holiness contained in the stones which are created by G-d.[45]

We must therefore say that the opposite is true. Despite the great advantage possessed by stones, bricks must contain an even greater quality. And because of that greater quality, the Egyptians so anxiously endeavored to make the Jews work (as their highest priority and for the most time) with bricks. For their intent was to introduce into the realm of *kelipah* the high spiritual level associated with bricks.

V. On the surface, it is possible to explain that the advantage possessed by bricks over stone (which, because of this advantage, the Egyptians desired to have the "storage cities for Pharaoh" built from bricks) is that their level is lower.

As is well known, "The Holy One, blessed be He, desired that He (blessed be He)[46] have a dwelling in the lower

---

43. [Trans. Note: The italics, in the original text, emphasize that the Egyptians appreciated the holiness of the Jewish people and sought to derive nurture from that potential as mentioned in sec. II and the sources cited there.]
44. Compare to *Tanya, Iggeres HaTeshuvah,* the conclusion of ch. 6.
45. To cite a parallel: In his *Shulchan Aruch, Hilchos Talmud Torah* 4:3, the Alter Rebbe writes that before a wicked person turns to G-d in *teshuvah,* the Torah and *mitzvos* he observes generate increased vitality in the realm of *kelipah.*
46. This parenthetic addition would frequently be made by the Rebbe Rashab. The intent is explained in *Likkutei Sichos,* Vol. XIX, p. 27ff.

realms."[47] As the Alter Rebbe (whose *yahrzeit* falls on Teves 24[48]) emphasizes,[49] this refers to [our material world], for "there is no lower level below it." Thus the lower the level that becomes a dwelling for G-d, the deeper and more consummate is the fulfillment of His will and intent. Thus building "the city of G-d" with bricks, which are on a lower level, fulfills G-d's intent more than building it with stones.[50]

To cite a parallel: The *Beis HaMikdash* possesses an advantage over the Sanctuary which accompanied the Jews in the desert. The Sanctuary was a temporary dwelling for G-d,[51] and was built primarily from (boards of) cedar, i.e., from the plant kingdom. The *Beis HaMikdash*, by contrast, is G-d's permanent dwelling[52] and it was built from stone,[53] inanimate matter, which is lower[54] than plants.[55]

---

47. *Midrash Tanchuma, Parshas Nasso*, sec. 16; see also *Bamidbar Rabbah* 13:6.
48. Which in the year of his passing, 5573, fell on *Motzo'ei Shabbos, Parshas Shmos*.
49. *Tanya*, ch. 36.
50. See *Menachos* 82a which states that "Any sacrifice that is obligatory may only be brought from non-sacred [animals]." [Animals which are consecrated — and thus holier — are not fit to be used.]
51. See *Shir HaShirim Rabbah* 1:16(3) which applies the verse (*II Shmuel* 7:6): "And I traveled in a tent," to the Sanctuary. (See also *Torah Or, Parshas Vayigash.*)
52. See *Shir HaShirim Rabbah, loc. cit.*, which applies the verse (*Tehillim* 132:14): "This is My resting place forever" to the *Beis HaMikdash*. (See also *Torah Or, loc. cit.*)
53. Indeed, it is forbidden to build with wood which projects outward in the *Beis HaMikdash* {*Rambam, Mishneh Torah, Hilchos Beis HaBechirah* 1:9 (this view is also accepted by the *Raavad*, see the gloss of the *Kessef Mishneh*) and *Sefer HaChinuch*, mitzvah 492, as cited in *Torah Or, loc. cit.*}.
54. The reason why the *Beis HaMikdash* was built with stones and not with bricks — although they are lower — is explained in note 95.
55. See the explanations in *Torah Or, loc. cit., Toras Chayim*, the *maamar* entitled *Vayigash*, sec. 8, and in the *Siddur*, p. 21b.
    In *Likkutei Torah, Devarim*, p. 99d, and in *Maamarei Admur HaZakein, Hanachos R. Pinchas*, p. 81, similar concepts are used to explain the advantage possessed by the Sanctuary of Shiloh over the Sanctuary in the desert. For in Shiloh, the walls were made of stone.*

---

* The standard text of *Likkutei Torah* states "curtains," but that is a printing error as noted by the Rebbe Rashab printed at the back of *Likkutei Torah*.

In truth, however, this explanation is not sufficient. If this was the higher quality that bricks possess (and thus it would be fitting to build "the city of our G-d" from bricks to fulfill G-d's intent for a dwelling in the lower worlds in a more consummate manner), the Egyptians (seeking to use the highest potentials the realm of holiness possesses for the purposes of *kelipah*) should have desired that the building of the cities for Pharaoh, the cities of *kelipah,* be performed only (by Jews) using bricks. It does not seem appropriate, however, for them to have forced the Jews to make bricks.

The fact that the Egyptians did compel the Jews to perform that activity — indeed, the fundamental element of their enslavement was directed toward that end[56] — indicates that making bricks expresses the ultimate advantage [of a Jew's service]. (And for that reason, the Egyptians compelled the Jews to make the bricks for Pharaoh's cities, so that they could derive nurture from the elevated effect produced by that activity.)

VI. The elevated quality which is brought out by making bricks can be understood through the preface of a more detailed explanation of the difference between the Sanctuary and the *Beis HaMikdash* stated above. [As mentioned,] the Sanctuary was made primarily from plants, while the *Beis HaMikdash* was built from stone.

Were it true that the Sanctuary did not include inanimate matter at all, one could say simply that it had not brought about a dwelling in the lower worlds. [For G-d's dwelling would not have encompassed] the realm of inanimate matter, the lowest rung possible (and that would not be achieved until the building of the *Beis HaMikdash*). In truth, however, the Sanctuary also included inanimate matter, for the floor of the Sanctuary was from earth. And the earth was an integral element of the Sanctuary as a

---

56. As reflected in the sources mentioned in note 7.

whole; it also contributed to the indwelling of G-d's Presence, as evident from the verse:[57] "And the priest will take from the earth on the floor of the Sanctuary."

As such, since G-dliness was drawn down to the lowest levels possible in the Sanctuary, why was the Sanctuary built from the plant kingdom instead of inanimate matter as was the *Beis HaMikdash*?

VII. The above concepts can be explained as follows: The elevated level that is achieved through drawing down G-dliness into the lower realms can be expressed in two ways:

a) Drawing G-dly light down in a manner which expresses its unlimited power, that it is infinite, and cannot be confined. It can even illuminate the lowest possible form of existence. (Were, by contrast, the light to be limited, it would not be able to extend that low.)

To cite a parallel [in the human realm]: a generous person. The greater his quality of generosity, the further he extends it, reaching out to people on lower levels. Avraham our Patriarch [can be pointed out as a paradigm]. His quality of kindness was so unbounded[58] that he granted influence to Arabs — who bowed down — to the dust on their feet.[59]

---

57. *Bamidbar* 5:17.

58. See *Torah Or* (the *maamar* entitled *Anochi Magen Loch*), p. 12a; the notes on this concept in *Likkutei Torah, LiGimmel Parshiyos*, p. 88a [see *Or HaTorah, Bereishis*, Vol. IV, p. 693a ff.].

59. *Bava Metzia* 86b; see also *Likkutei Sichos*, Vol. I, p. 28.

[Trans. Note: The analogy of light (also described in Chassidic terminology as *gilui milimaalah*, revelation from Above) implies a disadvantage. For the revelation does not permeate the lower realms as they exist within their own context. For example, when a window is opened and light enters a dark room, a fundamental change has not been made in the room itself. If the window is closed, it will be dark, just as it was previously. Similarly, in the analogue, the radiation of G-dly light in the Sanctuary, although G-d's light reached down to the level of the earth, it did not make a permanent change within the earth on which the sanctuary was erected. Indeed, once the Sanctuary was moved to another place, the earth remained ordinary, as it was before the Sanctuary had been erected. See note 77.

b) Through the fact that by drawing down G-dliness, His greatness is appreciated within the lower worlds. This expresses (not only the unlimited nature of the light, that it can be extended until the lowest levels, but also) the truth of G-dliness. This is reflected in the fact that created beings on a low spiritual plane (who are not G-dly) will also recognize Him.[60]

With regard to the *Beis HaMikdash*, in contrast, its construction brought about a permanent change in the nature of the place on which it was built. Therefore, even in the present age, thousands of years after the destruction of the *Beis HaMikdash*, its site is still holy, and must be treated with reverence (*Rambam, Mishneh Torah, Hilchos Beis HaBechirah* 6:16). This parallels the *motif* of *haalah milimatah limaalah*, elevation upward, in which created beings on the lower plane are elevated, refined, and brought close to G-dliness.]

60.   It can be explained that this reflects the distinction between the two reasons the *Etz Chayim* (*Shaar HaKlallim*) [gives for the creation of the world]: "to be generous to His created beings [reflecting the motif of revelation from Above] and so that they recognize His greatness."

This also reflects the distinction between the rationale "that they recognize His greatness," and [the reason for creation mentioned by] the *Zohar* (Vol. II, *Parshas Bo*, p. 42b): "so that He makes Himself known to them." For "so that He makes Himself known" (implies even against their will), i.e., that there be a revelation of G-dliness in the world. "So that He makes Himself known," follows the motif of revelation from Above, [i.e., independent of the refinement of the created beings, He reveals Himself to them].

{[The association of the rationale "so that He makes Himself known" with the motif of revelation from Above is also reflected in the *Etz Chayim* [*Shaar Alef*] (*Shaar HaHakdamos, Hakdamah* 3) [which mentions as a reason for creation]: "so that the perfection of His powers be revealed." From the statements of the *Etz Chayim* that "this rationale was already explained in the *Zohar*... also in *Parshas Bo*," one can conclude that the rationale ["so that the perfection of His powers be revealed"] shares the same general thrust as "so that He makes Himself known," [for both involve revelation from Above]. See also the *maamar* entitled *Yom Tov Shel Rosh HaShanah 5666*, and the *maamar* entitled *Shokav Amudei Sheish 5702*, sec. 18, which states that "so that the perfection of His powers be revealed" is an explanation of the *Zohar's* statement," so that He makes Himself known."}

In the above motif, however, the concept of willingly accepting His will is not relevant. With regard to "the created beings recogniz[ing] His greatness," the intent [and the focus] is on the created beings and their appreciation of His greatness so that they will merit to be a medium [for Him].

On this basis, we can appreciate why the reason given by the *Etz Chayim* in *Shaar HaHakdamos*, ["so that the perfection of His powers be revealed"] relates to the creation as a whole, while the explanation given in *Shaar HaKlallim* ["so that they recognize His greatness"] refers particularly to the

This new development, that created beings should recognize G-dliness, is a far greater (breakthrough and) advantage over the extension of G-dliness to this material plane. For in this second motif, the truth of G-dliness is expressed so powerfully that even another entity recognizes the truth. To borrow an expression coined by the *Ralbag*:[61] "The unique dimension of truth is that accord is reflected from every side."[62]

Since we are speaking about a recognition of the truth of G-dliness on the part of creations within our material frame of reference, it is clear that this recognition is achieved fundamentally and in the most consummate manner through developing an awareness of G-dliness from proofs derived from the nature of creation itself; ([this follows the motif of *haalah*] *mimateh limaalah*). For this demonstrates how the creation itself reflects the truth of G-dliness. Nevertheless, even when the awareness [on the part] of a created being comes as a result of a revelation of G-dly light from Above[63]

"emanation of one point that includes ten" (i.e., [the emanation of] the Ten *Sefiros* of the *Akudim* that were contained in one *keili*). For the rationale "so that they recognize His greatness" was consummated with the emanation of the *Akudim* (and not through the higher levels of Divine emanation), because the *Akudim* represent the beginning of the existence of *keilim* (the *maamar* entitled *HaSam Nafsheinu*, 5724) [see *Hemshech 5672*, Vol. II, p. 1119].

61. *Sefer Milchemes HaShem*, Discourse 6, the conclusion of ch. 15, cited in *Kitzurim VeHaaros LiTanya*, p. 102.

62. [Trans. Note: I.e., a truth is true. It is the reality and because of its truth, it will be reflected in every setting. To cite a basic example, within the context of the conceptual framework that prevails in our world, 2+2=4. No matter how hard someone will shout: "No, it equals 5," that will not change the reality. Taking the concept a step further: with regard to Einstein's theory, $e=mc^2$, the fact that for thousands of years, people were not aware of this reality did not alter it. Since this theory is true, its truth is reflected in the interplay of energy and matter to the extent that ultimately it could not help but be recognized.

And going further: since G-d is the true reality, even a frame of reference which outwardly does not recognize Him, and which defines existence in terms of its own conception, will ultimately come to the awareness of Him.]

63. [Trans. Note: In the motif of *haalaah milimatah limaalah*, the lower rung is elevated and lifted to a higher level. The classic example used to illustrate this mode is a student who studies and elevates his understanding. Once he

— in which instance the awareness has not permeated the created being's conceptual framework as powerfully — there is still an advantage to the fact that the G-dly light is appreciated and His truth recognized over the revelation of the light itself.[64] For the acceptance of influence [points to a higher and] deeper level than [the generation of] the influence itself.[65] To express this concept using the terminology of *Chassidus:* "The source of the *keilim* (the receptacles of Divine light) is higher than the source of the light."

---

has learned new concepts, he has changed himself; he now possesses a more developed intellectual potential than he did previously.

Within this level, there are two approaches: one student whose skills focus on his ability to recall his teacher's instruction. Since he has assimilated and internalized the wisdom he was taught, his own level has advanced. Nevertheless, his advance is due primarily to the influence received from his teacher. He has not changed his own thinking processes fundamentally.

The second approach is illustrated by a student who was taught not only to parrot his teacher, but to deal with new and different conceptual frameworks according to the mindset of his teacher. See *Likkutei Sichos*, Vol. X, p. 82, which explains similar concepts while interpreting *Avos* 2:9 which describes R. Eliezer ben Horkenus as "a cemented cistern which does not lose a drop," i.e., he preserves his teacher's wisdom, and R. Elazar ben Arach: "as a stream that flows with ever-increasing strength," i.e., he extends his teacher's wisdom to new and different situations concerning which he had not received instruction from him. These two approaches can be compared to the recognition of G-dliness because of a revelation from Above, and the recognition that stems from proofs derived from the nature of creation itself.]

64. [Trans. Note: I.e., even the student on the first level has changed his conceptual framework.]

65. This represents the further extension indicated by the expression "The culmination of deed [is] first in thought" (the *Lecha Dodi* hymn) over the "The beginning is implanted in the end" (*Sefer Yetzirah* 1:7). "The end" refers to the conclusion of the influence. In this level is implanted "the beginning," the very root of the influence. (As explained in the text, through drawing down G-d's light to the lowest levels, "the end ," its unlimited power, is revealed.)

"The culmination of deed," in contrast, refers to the acceptance of the influence. This level is "first in thought," i.e., preceding even the highest level of thought, above even the root of the influence (the *maamar* entitled *HaSam Nafsheinu, loc. cit.,* see also *Toras Chayim,* the *maamar* entitled *Vayigash,* chs. 2 and 3) [*Hemshech 5672,* Vol. II, p. 1119; *Likkutei Sichos,* Vol. XIX, p. 384ff.].

{[This concept can also be illustrated by] an analogy of a generous person.[66] His desire to do good for others comes (not only because of the want of the recipient, that he is in need of the giver's generosity, but also) as a result of his own nature. Since he is by nature a generous person, that nature seeks expression in giving and doing good for others.

To cite an example: When Avraham our Patriarch had no guests to whom to show hospitality, it caused him pain.[67] Since he was a generous person, his nature pushed him to do good.[68] Therefore, just as the expression of his nature through doing good brought him pleasure, when his attribute of kindness lacked expression, he felt discomfort.

Nevertheless, we see that when a generous person does a kindness to another person, and that person accepts [and recognizes] the kindness, this awakens a greater degree of satisfaction than that evoked by the giving itself. For, as stated above, the acceptance of influence [points to a higher and] deeper level than [the generation of] the influence itself.[69]}

---

66. See *Toras Chayim*, loc. cit., ch. 3.
67. *Rashi, Bereishis* 18:1; see also *Bereishis Rabbah* 48:9.
68. See the *maamar* entitled *HaChodesh HaZeh 5700*, sec. 3, and the *maamar* entitled *BaYom HaShemini 5708*, sec. 27, *et al.*
69. [Trans. Note: Through the analogy, the Rebbe is illustrating how in giving; there are two motifs functioning: the person's own desire to give — which parallels the revelation of Divine light from Above — and the relationship between the giver and the recipient — which reflects the advantage achieved through the recognition of G-d by the created beings.

When a person's giving is merely an expression of his nature, he is confined within his self. He is not concerned with the person to whom he is giving; even if the recipient is on a much lower level, he gives because his nature demands it. When, however, he becomes concerned with the recipient and how that person accepts the gift, he steps out of the limits of his own self and relates to that other person. This awakens within him greater satisfaction, because it brings out a deeper point in the soul, a level where there is no distinction between him and the other person. See *Likkutei Sichos*, Vol. VI, p. 116.

To cite a parallel: *Bava Basra* 9b: "Whoever gives a *perutah* to a poor person is granted six blessings, while one who appeases him with words is granted eleven blessings." When giving charity, one does not necessarily have to relate to the recipient. Appeasing him with words, by contrast, involves

VIII. The above reflects the difference between the Sanctuary and the *Beis HaMikdash*: The Sanctuary gave expression to the unlimited power of G-d's light, showing how it can be extended to the lowest possible levels, even to inanimate matter. The *Beis HaMikdash*, by contrast, reflected [a deeper step]: the beings of this material plane — even inanimate matter — became a medium for G-dliness.

For this reason, the Sanctuary was itself constructed in a manner which reflects [descent] from above downward. The roof of the Sanctuary was made from the hides of rams, *techashim*,[70] and goats, and their wool,[71] i.e., the animal kingdom. The walls ([wooden boards,] which were below the roof) were from the plant kingdom, and the floor of the Sanctuary was earth (inanimate matter). In the *Beis HaMikdash*, in contrast, an opposite motif was followed. The fundamental and primary element of the structure was [stone,] inanimate matter.[72] It was used to build the entire

---

communication and establishing a rapport with him; stepping beyond one's own self.

In the analogue, the revelation of light from Above reflects a dimension of G-dliness which is limited to His own nature, as it were, i.e., it is an expression of light which is defined as light and does not leave room for anything else. This light is drawn down to the lowest levels of existence, showing how even in such a framework, this light can prevail.

The recognition of G-dliness by the created beings, by contrast, reflects an unlimited dimension of G-dliness, that He has no bounds whatsoever — neither darkness, nor light — and therefore can be appreciated by a created being, even though that being "lives in darkness," i.e., feels separate from Him.]

70. [Trans. Note: A beautiful, multi-colored animal that existed only at that time (*Shabbos* 28a); alternatively, the ermine (*Jerusalem Talmud, Shabbos* 2:3). Note the commentaries to *Shmos* 25:5.]

71. The bottom-most curtain of the roof included one type of flax besides two types of wool (*Rashi, Shmos* 26:1). It is possible to explain that this reflects the function of an intermediary between one level (the roof) and another level (the boards). Similarly, the lowest point of the boards stood within sockets — inanimate matter, [which served as an intermediary between the boards and the earth].

72. A slight question might be raised because the roof of the *Beis HaMikdash* included "[wooden] panels and beams of cedar" (*I Kings* 6:9), i.e., [entities from] the plant kingdom. See, however, *Middos* 4:6 which states that the *Beis*

Beis HaMikdash. Although there was a sub-structure built with beams of cedar, this was only an auxiliary element,[73] necessary for support and the like.[74]

When the advantage of the lowest level is that it enables the infinite power of G-d's light to be expressed, showing that the light can be drawn down to such a low level (but not that this level itself [becomes a medium which] expresses that light), the lowest level receives the final phases, the nethermost levels, of the influence. [The rationale is that] since the motif follows the pattern of light being drawn down as a revelation from Above, it is drawn down to the higher levels first and then to the lower levels. The lower levels thus follow (also qualitatively) the higher levels. This is the pattern that was manifest in the Sanctuary.[75]

When, however, the higher quality is expressed through the lower level itself and ascending *its* becoming a medium for G-dliness [through] recognizing His greatness, it is apparent that the fundamental importance is the lowest

---

HaMikdash had a ceiling of mortar, stones, and cement above this. The passages from *Torah Or* and *Toras Chayim* cited in note 74 state: "The cedar beams in the ceiling were merely supports for the fundamental structure of the ceiling which was made from inanimate matter." And "[the beams] merely supported the roof." (See also *Maamarei Admur HaZakein 5565*, pp. 142, 144, 146.) Note also the passages from the *Siddur Im Dach* and *Likkutei Torah* cited in note 55 which state that the beams were sunken into the ceilings. This is not the place for further discussion of this matter.

73. See *Middos* 3:8 (according to the version of the text cited by most commentaries); *Kessef Mishneh* commenting on *Rambam, Mishneh Torah, Hilchos Beis HaBechirah* 1:9; the commentaries to the *Mishnah, Middos* 1:6, *et al.*

74. *Torah Or, Parshas Vayigash; Toras Chayim,* the *maamar* entitled *Vayigash,* ch. 8.

75. [Trans. Note: Since the revelation from Above does not bring about an internal change within the recipient, the levels and gradations within the system of the recipient remain unaltered, and therefore are respected, as it were, by the light which shines into the system. With regard to the motif of *haalah milimatah limaalah,* by contrast, since the lower levels are refined and elevated, they are no longer "lower," and they are fit to receive the light on a higher level.]

level.[76] Therefore the *Beis HaMikdash* [which expresses this motif] was made *primarily* of stone.[77]

IX. The *Beis HaMikdash* fulfilled the ideal that elements of this lowly world itself become vessels for G-dliness (and not only that the light is drawn down through them). Nevertheless, it did not accomplish the ultimate expression of a dwelling in the lower realms. It is only in the Future era, the Era of *Mashiach,* and more particularly, the Era of the Resurrection,[78] that this purpose will be consummated. The *Beis HaMikdash* was only "a microcosm of the World to Come,"[79] and not the ultimate expression of G-d's dwelling in the lower realms.[80]

These concepts can be understood through [the preface of the explanation of the well-known statement of the Alter Rebbe,[81] [when asked why G-d] "desired a dwelling in the lower realms" [answered]: "With regard to a 'desire,' you don't ask why."[82]

---

76. See *Toras Chayim, loc. cit.,* which states that the *Beis HaMikdash* revealed the motif, "The culmination of deed [is] first in thought" (see footnote 65).

77. This also explains why the Sanctuary served as only a temporary dwelling for G-d, while the *Beis HaMikdash* served as a permanent dwelling (see notes 51, 52). For when the revelation is only drawn down from Above, it does not permeate the internal makeup of the recipient to a great degree. (Note *Likkutei Torah, Vayikra,* p. 2b,c which states that an arousal from Above that comes on its own initiative and which is not followed by striving from below upward will not endure.)

78. *Tanya,* ch. 36.

79. *Torah Or, loc. cit. Toras Chayim, loc. cit.,* uses the expression "resembling the Future era." See also *Tanya, loc. cit.* which after stating that the ultimate revelation will come in the Era of *Mashiach,* states that in microcosm, this was revealed at the time of the giving of the Torah.

80. [Trans. Note: For as will be explained, the *Beis HaMikdash* reflected how entities which are fit to be mediums for G-dliness realized their purpose. This is not G-d's ultimate intent.]

81. Cited in the *maamar* entitled *Yom Tov Shel Rosh HaShanah 5666,* and the *maamar* entitled *Shokav Amudei Sheish 5702,* sec. 19.

82. [Trans. Note: I.e., we are speaking about a true desire, not something wanted for a reason, but something wanted solely because it is wanted.

We expect every created being to have a reason for its existence. Since it did not exist previously and was brought into being, it is logical that it was brought into being for a purpose, a reason that makes sense.

The intent is that G-d did not have a reason[83] why He wanted a dwelling in the lower worlds. It was a desire, as it were, something which is above having a reason.[84]

What being has no purpose for its existence, needs no reason to be? Only G-d.

He is, He was, and He will be. His existence is not brought into being from nothingness, but rather His is true existence, for He exists independently without a cause or reason for being.

He invested a dimension of His genuine being, as it were, into the creation, as the Rambam (Mishneh Torah, Hilchos Yesodei HaTorah 1:1) states: "From the truth of His Being came into existence all the beings." This is what our Sages meant by saying He "desired" creation, i.e., He invested something which is not reasonable or logical, an aspect that does not have a purpose or a cause, a dimension of His true Being, into the creation.]

83. [Although] the Zohar and the Etz Chayim (as mentioned in note 60) give reasons for the creation of the world, [these reasons do not represent the ultimate truth]. They are [merely] preparatory steps [necessary] to complete the purpose of a dwelling in the lower realms. For the concept of a dwelling is that {not only is the entire essence found within, but} the essence is found there in a revealed manner (see Likkutei Sichos, Vol. IV, p. 1054, where this concept is explained at length).

In order for the essence to be revealed, [motifs] associated with revelation "to be generous with His created beings" and "so that they recognize His greatness" are necessary. For the knowledge and recognition [of G-d that come as a result of these motifs] are preparatory steps for the revelation of G-d's essence.

{[To cite a parallel:] The love and fear [of G-d] reflect the revealed powers of the soul. [As such, they are removed from the essence of the soul, and are not fit mediums for the revelation of G-d's essence.] Nevertheless, they are "the ways of G-d," because they enable G-d's essence to be expressed in revelation, through the actual deed of the mitzvos (Likkutei Sichos, Vol. III, p. 956).

Or to cite another example: Bringing the world into existence is possible only through the potential of G-d's essence. Nevertheless, the medium which actually brings the world into being is G-d's light, as it is enclothed in the vessels (keilim) (Tanya, Iggeres HaKodesh, Epistle 20, p. 130b). [I.e., His essential desire is expressed through the light and the vessels which are revealed mediums.] For the fulfillment of the purpose of "a dwelling in the lower worlds," a dwelling for His essence, comes through (the preparatory phases of) "to be generous with His created beings" (which is brought into fulfillment by G-d's light) and "so that they recognize His greatness" (which is brought into fulfillment by the vessels).}

It is possible to explain that this order was reflected in the order of the indwelling of G-d's Presence. First, His Presence was manifest in the Sanctuary which reflected G-d's light, then in the Beis HaMikdash (built by Shlomo)

From this, it is understood that this dwelling in the
lower realms, which is the subject of G-d's desire (which is
above reason), does not reflect the attainment of a particular purpose or the attainment of fulfillment. For were this
to be the case, that purpose or fulfillment would be the reason for His wanting a dwelling. Instead, the intent is
something that cannot be considered as an advantage or the
attainment of fulfillment.[85] [There is no reason or logic for
it.] Only this can represent the true dwelling in the lower
realms in which the intent that G-d desired is expressed.

Therefore (in the Sanctuary and) in the *Beis HaMikdash*,
the true purpose of the dwelling in the lower realms which

---

which reflected the vessels, and the *Beis HaMikdash* to be built in the Future
which will be a dwelling for His Essence.

84.   These concepts are also reflected in our Divine service. If the world was created for a reason, the creation itself would have some importance, for it is the
medium which fulfills G-d's intent. As such, the person who carries out this
mission would also be given a certain degree of importance, [for it is his
service] who brings this intent to fruition.

Since the true purpose of the creation is that "this arose in His will" —
"He desired" — the creation has no importance or point of connection to
Him. For the entire purpose for its existence is that G-d desired it. [To
explain: Were there to be a reason and rationale for the creation, the world
and the person fulfilling that purpose would deserve recognition as representative of that purpose. It would symbolize something of genuine meaning and
importance.

Since, however, the world came about only because of a desire — and a
desire is not motivated by a valid reason — there is no reason for a person to
attach any importance to his accomplishment of G-d's desire. For even when
the desire is brought to fruition, the person has not accomplished anything
necessary or required. He has merely carried out a desire.]

Thus making a dwelling for Him comes through utterly negating and
nullifying the feeling of one's own importance. (The person should not think:
"I am important because I have fulfilled G-d's intent.") For the entire concept
of a dwelling in the lower realms is not something that it necessary. It is only
the subject of His desire (see note 93).

85.   From the fact that the intent for the dwelling in the lower realms stems from
G-d's essence which is above all revealed levels {for even the light which is a
revelation from His essence is for the sake of this intent (see the *maamar* entitled *ViAsisa Chag Shavuos, 5673*, and the *maamar* entitled *Anochi Havayah
E-lokecha 5703*, sec. 3}, it can be understood that it was His will and His
choice that motivated His desire, not a logical reason. For His essence is not
characterized by any description, nor does He have tendencies of any sort.

G-d desired was not manifest. For the dwelling [for G-d brought about by these structures] expressed a particular advantage[86] [— these structures brought into an expression a positive quality that is recognizable. {[In the Sanctuary,] G-d's light was drawn down even to the lowest levels, and} [in the *Beis HaMikdash*,] entities of this material world became a medium for G-dliness. [But the fact that the positive value of these achievements is recognizable indicates that this is not the dwelling His essence desired.]

X. Where is the ultimate expression of the dwelling in the lower worlds that "the Holy One, blessed be He, desired"?

In *Tanya*,[87] the Alter Rebbe explains that [His dwelling will be manifest] in [our material world], "the lowest level possible with regard to the concealment of [G-d's] light, a double and multiplied darkness to the extent that it is filled with *kelipos* and the *sitra achra* which are actually contrary to G-d, saying 'I am, and there is nothing else but me.'[88] [His dwelling will be manifest] in a place that has no connection with G-dliness. [It is not appropriate for G-dly light to shine there, and it is certainly not appropriate to become a medium for G-dliness.] On the contrary, it is filled with *kelipos* and the *sitra achra* whose existence is permeated by the feeling: "I am, there is nothing else but me."[89] Although

---

86. For these purposes, [i.e., the advantage these structures conveyed,] the explanation that G-d "desired" [a dwelling] is unnecessary. (For there is a rationale explanation [for the manifestation of His Presence].) Moreover, since they express an advantage and lead to fulfillment, they cannot fulfill the intent of G-d's desire, a dwelling [for His essence]. For since the dwelling is intended for His essence, as it were, the appreciation of the advantage and the fulfillment attained contradicts the revelation of His essence (see the preceding notes).

[The intent is that any intellectually sound reason, by definition, has a limited scope, for intellect must have bounds. As such, it is not a fit medium to express G-d's essence.]

87. Ch. 36.

88. Cf. *Yeshayahu* 47:8, 10; *Tzephaniah* 2:15.

89. [Trans. Note: The source for the feeling: "I am, there is nothing else but me," is G-d's essence, the only level that can aptly be described with such an expression. Every level of Divine light feels that it is an expression of the

they are the direct opposite of G-dliness and "are actually contrary to G-d," [it is] there [that] G-d desired to have His dwelling.

[The ultimate purpose is for] a Jew to take material entities which are "filled with *kelipos* and *sitra achra* which are contrary to G-d," and make a dwelling for G-d. [This is accomplished] (not through revealing the good and holiness which is latently concealed within them [— this is not possible, because —] their entire existence is "actually contrary to G-d,"[90] but rather) through breaking them and negating the *sitra achra* entirely. In this manner, the dwelling for G-d is established as a new creation through the Divine service of the Jewish people alone.[91] This is the dwelling desired[92] by the Holy One, blessed be He.[93]

Source of light and is therefore, nullified to that source. The *kelipos* which permeate our material world, by contrast, do not feel G-d's Presence and only feel themselves. Nevertheless, the possibility for them to have such a feeling stems from the fact that His essence is the source of their being.]

90. [Trans. Note: Certainly, in every element of existence, there is a spark of G-dliness. Indeed, without that spark of G-dliness, the entity could not continue to exist (*Tanya, Shaar HaYichud VehaEmunah*, ch. 1). Nevertheless, since our world is governed by the gestalt of *kelipah*, G-dliness invested in these entities is not evident, nor can it be revealed in a natural manner. To borrow an analogy from the laws of *kashrus*, the condition of the G-dly spark can be described with the expression *chatichah naaseh neveilah*: the substance though originally kosher, through its contact with an unkosher substance, is now considered as carrion. It is only, as the *sichah* continues to explain, through the Divine service of the Jewish people and the power to bring about a totally new change which G-d granted them that this G-dliness can be granted expression.]

91. On this basis, we can understand our Sages' statements (*Shabbos* 119b, *Shulchan Aruch HaRav* 268:1) that "Whoever prays on Friday night and recites the passage VaYichulu is considered as if he is a partner with the Holy One, blessed be He, in the task of creation."

The *Chidushei Aggados* of the *Maharsha* (*loc. cit.*) interprets this passage as follows: "By reciting VaYichulu, [the person] gives testimony about [G-d's] work of creation (see *Shulchan Aruch HaRav, loc. cit.*:12). By doing so, he becomes the partner of the Holy One, blessed be He, because without the person's testimony, G-d's work [of creation] would not be known."

On the surface, explanation is necessary: A person through his testimony makes known G-d's work of creation, but he does not add anything to the actual task of creation. How can he justly be called a partner to the Holy One, blessed be He, who created all existence?

[Based on the above explanations, this question can be resolved.] For a created being to "recognize G-d's greatness" {— the term "greatness" refers to the task of creation (*Berachos* 58a) —}, it is necessary for him to bring about an entirely new development, [one equal to G-d's creation of something from nothing]. [For man's recognition of the G-dliness present within the world despite the gestalt of *kelipah* is as radical a change as G-d's creation of the world from absolute nothingness.]

{[In this context, a *halachic* comparison can be made. In Jewish law, for a legal document to be considered viable, two types of witnesses are required: a) witnesses who sign the legal document, testifying to the truth of its contents, and b) *eidei kiyum,* witnesses who verify the signatures of the witnesses to the document.]

Similarly, in this context, by reciting *VaYichulu,* the person serves as an *eid kiyum* (without whose testimony, the legal document would have no power). Through these witnesses testimony, they establish [the authenticity of the legal document] and cause it to be considered a [significant] entity.}

The reason our Sages use the expression "is considered [a partner]," [i.e., and not "becomes a partner,] is that the potential to recognize G-dliness comes from G-d's essence (as will be explained in the text and in note 98) [and is thus not entirely the person's own contribution].

There is another concept implied. The *kelipos* and the *sitra achra* are entities without substance, non-beings (מציאות דהעדר) (*Toras Sholom,* p. 134ff.). Thus through the Divine service of subduing the *sitra achra* and transforming the darkness to light, a new development is brought about within the creation. [Entities that are] non-beings are transformed into entities of substance.

On this basis, we can appreciate the expression "partner in the task of creation," which implies that the person's activities have an effect on the creation itself (the existence of the heaven and the earth).

92. As it is written (cf. *Iyov* 14:15; see *Shmos Rabbah* 36:4, *Vayikra Rabbah* 31:1): "He desired the work of your hands."

Kesubos 5a applies the expression: "The deeds of the righteous are greater than the making of heaven and earth" to the Sanctuary and to the *Beis HaMikdash.* And in the *maamar* entitled *Gedolim Maaseh Tzaddikim 5685,* sec. 7, it is explained that the advantage of the deeds of the righteous is reflected in the new development brought about by the nullification of *yesh* (self-conscious existence) to *ayin* (nothingness). {See also *Shmos Rabbah* (*loc. cit.*) which explains that the expression "He desires the work of your hands" as referring to the service in the Sanctuary.}

Nevertheless, since the holiness drawn down in the Sanctuary and the *Beis HaMikdash* does not reach the lowest levels of existence themselves (those which are "filled with the *kelipos* and the *sitra achra*"), this cannot be considered as an entirely new development. {To cite a parallel, the *maamar* entitled *Tiku 5667* (in the series of *maamarim* entitled *Yom Tov Shel Rosh HaShanah 5666;* see also the *maamar* entitled *Acharei 5666*) explains that the

And this — to make a dwelling for G-d even in a place where the created beings are "actually contrary to G-d" has no place in logic,[94] and it is not within the potential of the revealed levels of G-dliness.[95] For it is impossible to have an

---

task of refinement carried out through drawing down Divine light cannot truly be considered as a new development.} Thus [the service in the Sanctuary and the *Beis HaMikdash*] cannot be considered the ultimate expression of "the deeds of the righteous" (man's Divine service). [That will not come until the service during the exile will bear fruit in the construction of the Third *Beis HaMikdash*.]

See also *Rashi's* commentary to *Shmos* 15:17: "The Sanctuary of G-d, established by Your hands," [which notes that the phrase uses the plural "hands" and states: "When will the Sanctuary be built with two hands?... In the Future (i.e., the Era of the Redemption)." And *Kesubos, loc. cit.*, derives the concept "The deeds of the righteous are greater" from that prooftext.

93. Although this dwelling is fashioned through the Divine service of mortals, there is no personal sense of pride involved (see note 84). A parallel can be drawn to the advantage possessed by "a simple servant" over "a faithful servant," as described in the *maamar* entitled *Acharei 5666*. Although the service of a simple servant is an entirely new development which is achieved through his own initiative alone, his work is, nevertheless, identified as his master's (and indeed, this identification is what makes this dynamic possible). For a (simple) servant does not view himself as an independent entity at all, as explained at length in that source.

From the fact that the dwelling is being established for G-d's essence, as explained in note 96, we can appreciate that the *bittul* (self-nullification) required is of a more consummate level than the *bittul* involved in Divine service that is motivated by the revealed levels of G-dliness. For the *bittul* involved in Divine service that is motivated by the revealed levels of G-dliness [is incomplete], as reflected by the statement (cf. *Zohar*, Vol. I, p. 11b): "Everything before Him is as nothing," i.e., because of one's awareness of G-d's greatness, one considers oneself as nothing. [Implied is that the person retains a certain vestige of self; for indeed, it is he who perceives G-d's greatness and therefore concedes his self-importance.] The *bittul* evoked by G-d's essence, by contrast, [is total], as reflected by the verse (*Devarim* 4:39): "There is nothing else," [i.e., one feels that there is no existence whatsoever apart from G-dliness] (the *maamar* entitled *U'Lekachtem Lachem*, 5661, and the *maamar* entitled *Im Bechukosai 5667*).

94. [Trans. Note: For there is no reason to make a dwelling for G-d in a place that is entirely unsuitable for that purpose.]

95. The creation of the lower realms of existence was not motivated by a reason. {For as explained at the beginning of the series of *maamarim* entitled *Yom Tov Shel Rosh HaShanah 5666* and the *maamar* entitled *Shokav 5702*, the reasons mentioned by the *Zohar* and the *Etz Chayim* do not necessitate the creation of the worlds of *Beriah*, *Yetzirah*, and *Asiyah*, and certainly, do not necessitate the creation of our material world.} Similarly, the ultimate motive for the revela-

effect in such a place through drawing down G-dly light or even through the source of the *keilim* (for these levels cannot become vessels for G-d's] light, as explained above). [The transformation of such a place into a dwelling for Him] is possible only through the power from G-d's essence alone[96] (for it was He who desired to have this dwelling); "He alone has the power and the potential to create some-

---

tion of G-dliness in these realms is not motivated by these rationales. For since the lower realms were not brought into being because {of the rationales stemming from} the revealed levels of G-dliness, these revealed levels of G-dliness do not affect them.

On this basis, we can appreciate why (at the outset), the *Beis HaMikdash* had to be built from stone. For the new development of the *Beis HaMikdash* (over the Sanctuary) was that the entities of the lower realms became vessels for G-dliness, as explained in sec. VIII. Since bricks are lower than stones, seemingly it would have been proper to build the *Beis HaMikdash* with bricks rather than stones, because they are on a lower level. This was not done, because the revelation of the *Beis HaMikdash* could not penetrate to the bricks. For as explained above, bricks represent the side of impurity. (See *Tanya*, ch. 7, which states that when a person eats without an intent to elevate the food, his eating "is not better... than the *kelipos* and the *sitra achra* in this world;... which are in the majority — indeed to the extent that one can say entirely — evil," [i.e., *kelipah* permeates the gestalt of our world and thus bricks are unfit for the *Beis HaMikdash*].)

Although if there were no stones available, the *Beis HaMikdash* could be built with bricks (*Rambam, Hilchos Beis HaBechirah, 1:8*); such a brick building would relate to the level of bricks that resembles stone. (As the passage from *Tanya* cited previously continues, [in *kelipas nogah*,] there is "a small amount of good mixed together with it.")

Note the explanation in the series of *maamarim* entitled *Matzah Zu 5640*, sec. 60, with regard to the advantage of the Chanukah lamps (which we are commanded to place at the entrance to our homes, at the outside) over the study of the Torah, [i.e., that the Chanukah lamps elevate the public domain].

With regard to Torah study, it is also said (*Devarim 6:7*): "And you shall speak of them ... when you walk on your way." Nevertheless, even in such a situation, Torah study does not draw light into the public domain, the "separate mountains" (cf. *Tanya*, end of ch, 33), to the same extent as the Chanukah lamps do. For the obligation to speak the words of Torah "when you walk on your way" comes in continuation — and thus resembles — the obligation to speak words of Torah when "you sit at home."

96. Moreover, the dwelling established in the lower worlds is a dwelling for G-d's essence. And as explained in several sources, in His dwelling, His entire essence is found.

thing from nothing and absolute non-being."[97] And He transferred, as it were, that power to the Jewish people so that they can make a dwelling for Him in the lower realms, despite this being an entirely new development, as explained above.[98]

XI. On this basis, we can appreciate the reason why the Jews' primary task in Egypt was making bricks. The way bricks are made is that after the prepared cement is poured into the mold used to form the bricks, they are placed into a fiery furnace[99] where they harden and become as strong as stone. As it is written with regard to the generation who built the Tower of Bavel:[100] "Let us make bricks and burn them in a fire, and the bricks will be as stone," i.e., it is through "burn[ing] them in fire," that the bricks become "as stone." [The fire] gives the bricks the hardness and strength that stones (creations made by G-d) [inherently] possess and enables one to use [the bricks] to build a structure (of holiness).[101]

Since the strength which the bricks possess comes from burning them in fire, we can apply the law stated with regard to an earthenware utensil:[102] After it is burned in a kiln, it is considered as a new entity.[103]

---

97. *Tanya, Iggeres HaKodesh*, Epistle 20 (p. 130b).
98. Note the *maamar* entitled *Tiku 5667*. There it states that the souls that descend to this physical plane (— they correspond to the level of a simple servant described above —) possess the power "to refine the complete material obsession that characterizes the animal soul — a task which is an entirely new development, equivalent to the creation of being from nothingness — [which] stems from the power of G-d's essence which has the potential to create being from nothingness."
99. See *Rashi, Bereishis* 11:3 (note also *Rashi, Shmos* 5:7). See also *Torah Or*, p. 77c ff.
100. *Bereishis* 11:3. As is stated in many sources (see those mentioned in note 24, *Or HaTorah, Parshas Shmos*, p. 24, the *maamar* entitled *Zos Chanukas 5640*, ch. 14, the subjugation of the Jewish people and their efforts in making bricks corrected the sin of making the bricks for the Tower of Bavel.
101. *Torah Or, loc. cit.*
102. [This is relevant with regard to the laws of ritual purity and impurity, as stated by] *Tosafos* (*Pesachim* 30b, entry *HaTorah; Zevachim*, 96a, entry *Ela*); see

The strength the bricks possess is {not an innate tendency which the person is revealing,} but rather a new potential which is brought about primarily through the person's activity in burning the bricks and negating their previous form of existence.

Therefore making bricks (when this is done with the intent of using them to build "the city of our G-d") represents [the Jews'] task in making a dwelling for G-d in the lower realms. For the making of bricks involves two phases:

a) burning and negating the previous form of the bricks which stems from "the side of impurity,"[104] and

b) making them hard and strong as stone, infusing them with the strength of holiness possessed by stones which are made by G-d. [Endowing bricks with] this strength is a totally new development which is brought about through the labor of a mortal.

Parallels to these two phases are found in the mission of creating a dwelling in the lower worlds:

a) This is achieved through breaking and negating the *kelipos* and *sitra achra* of which the world is full, and

b) This is an entirely new creation which is brought about through man's Divine service.

For this reason, the fundamental task of the Jewish people throughout exile, beginning with the Egyptian exile,

---

also *Rambam, Mishneh Torah, Hilchos Keilim* 1:6, 13; 15:1, *et al.*

103. The same concepts apply with regard to bricks. [They are also considered as new entities, different entirely from their previous state.]

These concepts can also be applied with regard to man (who creates this dwelling for G-d). Since "his foundation is earth" (Yom Kippur liturgy), [he is also an earthenware utensil]. There is no way of correcting his material inclination {i.e., his tendencies to undesirable character traits which he has to a greater extent than animals (*Kuntres U'Mayon*, Discourse 15, ch. 2)}. They must be burnt, nullifying his *yeshus* (self-consciousness) [entirely].

A parallel [can be made to the laws of *kashering*] an earthenware utensil. Boiling is not sufficient. It must be burned in fire. See the *maamar* entitled *VeAfu* (*Likkutei Torah, Vayikra,* p. 48c).

104. See the sources mentioned in note 35.

(the source for all [subsequent] exiles,[105]) involves making bricks. Since the consummation of the dwelling for G-d in the lower realms that will be manifest in the Era of *Mashiach* and the Era of the Resurrection is "dependent on our deeds and Divine service throughout the duration of the exile,"[106] our work must resemble [its purpose]. Therefore our work throughout the exile involves "making bricks."

Everything in the world begins in the Torah, [described as] "the Torah of life." [Occupying ourselves in] ליבון הלכתא the clarification of Torah law, [takes the place of making bricks (לבנים).][107] Through these efforts, we will merit [a new revelation of] Torah, "the revelation of *P'nimiyus HaTorah* in the Era of the Redemption, [when] 'I will show you wonders[108].'"[109] This will lead to [new revelations in the world], [bringing] the world to consummate perfection, [manifesting the purpose of] its creation,[110] for G-d's dwelling in the lower worlds will be complete. [This will come to fruition with] the coming of *Mashiach*. May it be in the immediate future.

105. The *maamar* entitled *Kol Dodi 5709;* see *Bereishis Rabbah* 16:4.
106. *Tanya,* ch. 37.
107. *Raaya Mehemna* (*Zohar,* Vol. III, p. 153a), *et al.,* quoted and explained in *Torah Or,* the beginning of *Parshas Shmos,* and *Toras Chayim* and *Or HaTorah.*

    The clarification of Torah law parallels the two thrusts reflected in making bricks:

    a) the clarification of the laws comes through the removal and the weakening of the power of *kelipah* which veils and conceals the laws (see *Tanya, Iggeres HaKodesh,* Epistle 26, p. 144b ff.);

    b) through the clarification of Torah law, new Torah concepts are developed (see *Tanya, loc. cit.,* the *maamarim* entitled *Ashreichem Yisrael* and *Lech Lecha 5667*).
108. Cf. *Michah* 7:15.
109. *Torah Or, loc. cit.*
110. See *Tanya,* ch. 36; *Zohar,* Vol. III, p. 125a (note *Zohar,* Vol. I, p. 139a); *Rambam, Mishneh Torah,* the conclusion of *Hilchos Melachim; Avodas HaKodesh,* Vol. II, ch. 39.

Parshas Beshallach

Likkutei Sichos, Vol. VI, p. 86ff.

I. On the verse:[1] "And towards morning, the sea turned back to its power," the *Midrash*[2] states that when G-d created the sea, He established a condition [for its existence] with it: that it should split for the Jewish people when they desired to pass through. This is alluded to by the term לאיתנו, "to its power," whose letters can be rearranged to form the word לתנאו,[3] "as per its condition", i.e., the sea turned back to its power; it turned [back] because of the condition established with it at the outset.

There is, however, a conceptual difficulty. The verse "And... the sea turned back to its power" speaks, (not about the splitting of the sea, but on the contrary,) about what transpired afterwards when the sea returned to the state it was in before it split. How then can the *Midrash* associate the return of the sea "to its power" with the condition which G-d established with it at the outset?

The commentaries[4] answer that the condition that G-d stipulated with the sea (that it should split for the Jewish people) was that if it did not split for the Jews, it would never contain water again. {As Rabbi Pinchas ben Yair told the river *Ginei* (when the river refused to split for him):[5] "If

---

1. *Shmos* 14:27.
2. *Bereishis Rabbah* 5:5; *Shmos Rabbah* 21:6; *Zohar*, Vol. II, p. 198b.
3. *Baal HaTurim* to the verse.
4. *Yedei Moshe* to *Bereishis Rabbah, loc. cit.*
5. *Chullin* 7a. See also *HaYom Yom*, p. 20 (referring to the statement of the Maggid of Mezeritch cited in sec. II) that the splitting of the river *Ginei* was a

you do not split for me, I will decree that water will never pass through you again."}

On that basis, they explain the statement of the *Midrash* that the return of the sea to its power reflected the fulfillment of its condition. For if it had not fulfilled its condition, its existence would have been nullified entirely.

This resolution is, however, not entirely satisfactory [for the following reasons]:[6]

a) Had the sea not fulfilled its condition (not only would it not have had any strength, it would have ceased to exist entirely). As *Rashi* indicates, however, the word לאיתנו, only alludes to the sea's power, [not to the totality of its existence]. [Why then is its power associated with the fulfillment of its condition?]

b) The literal interpretation of the word לתנאו is "to its condition," the sea turned back to its condition. According to the above interpretation, by contrast, it appears that the sea turned back to its power because it fulfilled the condition established with it. The returning itself, however, does not involve its condition.

II. There is a *maamar* in the text *Or Torah* that was collected from the Maggid of Mezeritch's teachings (which he in turn attributes to the Baal Shem Tov[7]) that focuses on the verse: "And towards morning, the sea turned back to its power." The Maggid also focuses on the association of the sea's "power" and the condition established with it as stated by the *Midrash*. Using this *Midrash*, {he explains the expression used by our Sages:[8] "fulfilling the will of the Omnipresent,"

---

microcosm of the splitting of the Red Sea. See *Chullin, ibid.,* which compares Rabbi Pinchas to Moshe and the 600,000 Jews.

6. Similar questions can be raised concerning the resolution the *Or HaChayim* (in his commentary to the above verse) offers to this difficulty.

7. *HaYom Yom, loc. cit.*

8. *Berachos* 35b.

rather than fulfilling His word or His utterance,[9] and also}
the answer given by Rabbi Pinchas ben Yair to the river
Ginei mentioned above: "If you do not split for me, I will
decree that water will never pass through you again."

Since G-d established a condition with the entire creation[10] "that it carry out the will of the righteous even
though it is against its nature," if the river *Ginei* had not
fulfilled the condition by splitting, "it would be as if it had
never existed at all, as if water had never been created
there. And thus water would never pass through it again."
In other words, by stating that "water will never pass
through you again," Rabbi Pinchas ben Yair was stating
more than that the river would be dry in the future. His
intent was that since the river was created on the condition
that it fulfill the will of the righteous, its entire existence,
including its existence up until that time, was dependent on
its fulfillment of the condition. For if it had not fulfilled
"the condition stipulated at the time of the utterance
[which brought it into being]," it would have been as if "it
had never been created at all." For it would never have
existed in such a manner.

On this basis, we can explain the difficulty raised above:
that had the sea not split for the Jews, not only would it
have lost its power, its entire existence would have ceased.

The sea's fulfillment of the condition had an effect
beyond securing its continued existence (for had it not
fulfilled the condition, water would not have flown through
it again). {Although it is seemingly inappropriate to say that

---

9. [Trans. Note: G-d's word or His utterance refers to the creative power that
enclothes itself within the natural order and maintains its existence. For the
natural order was established through His speech at the beginning of creation. His will refers to a higher level of G-dly light which is not confined in
this manner.]

10. See *Bereishis Rabbah, loc. cit.* (and the *Zohar, loc. cit.*) which state that "the Holy
One, blessed be He, did not establish a condition with the sea alone, but with
everything that was created during the six days of creation." See also the
commentary of the *Or HaChayim* mentioned above.

an entity that has already existed could be nullified [to the extent that it never existed],} had the sea not fulfilled the condition, even its existence until that time would have been nullified. [It would be] nullified as if it had never existed as [an element of] the creation,[11] (to the extent that it would have been "nothingness [12]and non-being as it actually was before[13] the six days of creation"[14]).

---

11. This is the wording used in *Or Torah, loc. cit.*

12. The wording is borrowed from the Alter Rebbe, *Tanya, Shaar HaYichud VehaEmunah*, ch.1, (when speaking about what would happen if "the letters [of G-d's speech which brought the world into being] would withdraw, Heaven forbid, even for a moment and return to their source"). See also the following note.

13. It is possible to explain the above concept as follows: Even the view which accepts that the created beings could exist independently (after they were brought into being, Heaven forbid, like a utensil which exists after having been fashioned by a craftsman — the error made by those who deny G-d's existence, as stated in *Tanya, Shaar HaYichud VehaEmunah*, ch. 2) would agree that G-d could make them into "absolute nothingness and non-being."

{When an entity is nullified through the activity of a created being, it is only the form [— and not the very core —] of the entity which is nullified. When, by contrast, G-d [nullifies an entity], even these opinions would agree that it could be nullified entirely. For it is understandable (see *Moreh Nevuchim*, Vol. II, ch. 17), that just as He can create something from nothing, so too, it is within His potential, to return that entity to nothingness. (This would be possible, even if the creation were, Heaven forbid, an independent entity. [For G-d would be a stronger and more powerful entity.])}

Nevertheless, in such an instance, since — as it exists in its own right — the entity would continue to exist, and the fact that it is nullified comes from a different [and higher] power, [G-d] — it cannot be said that it would be nullified to the extent that it is "nothingness and non-being as it actually was before the six days of creation," for then it had been an entity at the outset.* [In other words, since the entity existed, and, until it was nullified, had a right to exist, its nullification would affect only its future existence.]

By contrast, the entire being of the creation, even during the time when it does exist, [does not exist by virtue of its own power,] but comes about only as a result of the G-dly energy which brings it into being at all times. When that energy is withdrawn, its existence will be nullified as a matter of course. Thus (after the energy is withdrawn), the entity will not exist at all, in exactly the same [state of non-being as it was] before the six days of creation. (To cite a parallel: a stone that is propelled upward because of the energy [invested in it by the person who throws it]. As that energy dissipates, the stone will return to the earth as it was beforehand.**) [This said,] explanation is still necessary. See *Moreh Nevuchim*, Vol. I, ch. 69.

Therefore [the fulfillment of] the condition is associated with the power of the sea. Through the fulfillment of the condition, not only did the sea continue to exist afterwards

---

[Trans. Note: The conceptual difficulty which the Rebbe feels has not been totally resolved is the question: How can an entity which has existed be considered as if it never existed at all? Valid distinctions can be made between the existence of the world and its non-being when compared to any other transition between states of being; still, our understanding of existence prevents us from appreciating how an object which was can cease to be entirely.]

---

* A further point can be made: According to this opinion, it could be said that the world was created only for a limited time, 6000 years, and after that time it will be nullified entirely. (This shows that even during the time in which the world exists, it is not a genuine entity, see sec. V.) Nevertheless, if this entity (even though it is not genuine) would exist on its own accord (without having to be renewed continuously by the Creator), even after its existence was nullified — although that nullification would come as a matter of course, the existence of that entity would not [— in an abstract sense —] be utterly void. It could not be described as being exactly what it was before the six days of creation.

** Furthermore, with regard to the example of throwing a stone, it is appropriate afterwards to say that at the outset, the stone had been projected upward. In the analogue, [the existence of our world,] since time itself is a created entity (see *Derech Mitzvosecho, Mitzvas HaAmanas Elokus*, ch. 11, *et al.*), if (the utterance enclothed within [a particular creation] from) the Ten Utterances of Creation would be withdrawn, time would also cease. And thus no trace of its existence would remain at all. Further explanation is, however, still required.

14. It is possible to explain that the nullification of the existence of the sea, were it not to have fulfilled its condition, {and similarly, the nullification of the existence of the entire creation if the Jews would not have accepted the Torah (*Shabbos* 88a, *Avodah Zarah* 3a)} would have been greater than the nullification [of the existence of the creation] that would come about "were the letters [of the Ten Utterances] to withdraw, Heaven forbid, even for a moment" as mentioned in *Shaar HaYichud VehaEmunah, loc. cit.*

With regard to the withdrawal of the letters, [it could be explained that] the existence of the world until the moment when the letters withdrew (could be considered an existence according to the Torah, because of the Ten Utterances through which the world was created), and its nullification affects only the future. (When, however, the existence would be nullified, it would be nullified as if it had never existed before, as explained in the previous note.) With regard to [the nullification of the existence of the sea were it not to have fulfilled its condition,] since it was brought into existence conditionally, if that condition was not fulfilled, [the existence of the sea] would have been nullified retroactively. See also note 40.

(without change), [but] strength and power was endowed to its previous existence.[15]

This explanation, however, resolves only the first difficulty — why the verse states לאיתנו, which indicates that the fulfillment of the condition effected only the sea's power, because [the splitting effected] (also[16]) the previous existence of the sea. The second question — that the meaning of the word לתנאו is "to its condition" — appears to be unresolved. For the sea did not return "to its condition."

III. The resolution of the above can be understood by prefacing the explanation of the difficulty in the meaning of the term לאיתנו, "to its power," which required the *Midrash* to interpret it as לתנאו, is "to its condition."[17]

The fact that the Torah tells us that the sea returned לאיתנו, "to its power," is obviously a new development. [For otherwise, it would not have been necessary to say so. Yet that raises a question:] Why would we think that the fact that G-d "transformed the sea into dry land"[18] weakened the nature of the sea to the extent that even when the sea returned, it no longer had its original strength? Why must the Torah state לאיתנו, "to its power," to negate such a conception?

---

15. See a similar explanation which is offered in *Or HaTorah, Vaes'chanan*, p. 415ff.
16. Obviously, even according to this explanation, the verse also refers to the existence of the sea from this point onward (not only the strength endowed to its existence until its splitting). Therefore the verse mentions "to its power" after stating "and the sea returned" although the strength was endowed to its previous existence when it fulfilled its condition, and not when it "returned."
17. The *Maharzav* (in his commentary to *Shmos Rabbah, loc. cit.*) states that the verse should have said that the sea returned to its previous state (לקדמותו) or to its strength (לתקפו). The fact that it uses the term לאיתנו, "to its power," leads the *Midrash* to interpret it as לתנאו is "to its condition."

  Nevertheless, as explained above, not only the choice of wording, but the very fact that the Torah adds a word that appears unnecessary is what arouses the question.
18. *Shmos* 14:21.

One might be able to resolve these questions through explaining that we find {[in general, and] in particular, in connection with the exodus from Egypt,} two types of miracles:[19]

a) Miracles which change the nature [of the entities] which existed previously, for example, the miracle in which Moshe inserted his hand in his bosom and it came out "leprous like snow."[20] After the miracle, Moshe's hand remained leprous; that became its natural state. For it to return to a state of health,[21] a second miracle was necessary to negate the leprosy.[22]

b) Miracles in which the situation created by the miracle remains miraculous, defying nature; for example, the miracle of the transformation of the water into blood. The water remained water; its nature did not change. It is just that [for the Egyptians], its apparent and functional state was blood.[23] Therefore, when the miracle ceased, [another miracle was not necessary to transform the blood back to water]. On the contrary, the change to blood was nullified as a matter of course.[24]

With regard to the matter at hand, the miracle of the splitting of the sea: If the transformation of the sea to dry land meant that the nature of the water changed and it actually became land, the return of the sea would require

---

19. See *Likkutei Sichos*, Vol. V, pp. 175-176 and notes where this concept is explained at length.
20. *Shmos* 4:6.
21. *Ibid.*:7.
22. This is also reflected in our Sages' statement (*Shabbos* 97a) and *Rashi's* commentary to that verse. See also *Shmos Rabbah*, ch. 3:13 which states that this indicates that a positive attribute will be expressed more rapidly than an attribute of retribution.
23. To the extent that if there was a barrel full of water, a Jew would be able to drink water from it, but for an Egyptian, it would be blood unless he purchased the water from a Jew (*Shmos Rabbah* 9:10).
24. And thus, it was not necessary to empty the ponds, the reservoirs, and the containers in which the water which had turned into blood had been collected.

making a new entity, [making the land, sea]. Therefore the verse states: "the sea turned back to its power," indicating that it returned to the strength which it originally possessed, as *Rashi* states: "to its original power."[25] For even when it was outwardly dry land, it remained (in its inner state), water.[26]

This interpretation is, however, not sufficient. From the fact that the miracle of the splitting of the sea came about because "G-d propelled the entire sea with a strong east wind throughout the entire night,"[27] it is evident that the sea did not undergo a fundamental change in nature and become dry land. {The fact that the water "stood like a column and like a wall"[28] came about through (the Divine

---

25. According to the explanation above, it is clear why *Rashi* adds the word "original," although the meaning of לאיתנו is (only) "to its power."* For this explains the new concept brought out by the verse "the sea turned back to its power."

   * One cannot say, however, that *Rashi's* intent in adding the word "original" is to interpret the verse "And the sea *returned* to its power" because (in addition to the fact that this concept can be understood even without *Rashi's* commentary), *Rashi* cites only the word לאיתנו as the source for his interpretation.

26. [To state a parallel:] In Jewish law (*Sukkah* 30b, *Bava Kama* 96b), we find the concept that "a change which will revert to its original state (even if it has not yet returned to that state) is not considered a change." And this applies even when an activity is required to return it to that state.

27. *Shmos* 14:21. This demonstrates that as *Tanya, Shaar HaYichud VehaEmunah*, ch. 2, states: "If G-d would have stopped the wind for a moment, the water would have returned and flowed downward as is its natural pattern."
   Based on what is stated above, it is understood why the Alter Rebbe found it necessary to cite the fact that G-d caused the wind to blow all night (and were He to have paused for a moment, the water would have reverted to its ordinary pattern) as proof that [the miracle was ongoing in nature]. He did not prove this from the actual fact that as soon as the wind stopped, the sea reverted to its natural state. For the returning of the sea is not indisputable proof [of the miracle's ongoing nature]. For (were it not for the concept derived from the word לאיתנו), it is possible to say that the water's reversion to its natural state came as a result of an activity (a [second] miracle), and did not come about as a matter of course.

28. *Tanya, Shaar HaYichud VehaEmunah, loc. cit.*
   The wording of the Alter Rebbe communicates a new concept. On the surface, there is a difficulty. [The word נד, rendered as "column," in our translation of the passage from *Tanya*,] is also found in *Shmos* 15:8. There the

power that enclothed itself[29] in) the east wind that continued blowing the entire time.} [Had that wind stopped, the

---

Targum, Rashi, and others interpret נד as "a wall." Accordingly, several questions arise with regard to the Alter Rebbe's choice of wording:

a) Seemingly, his wording is redundant, for "like a נד, and like a wall"
[share the same meaning];

b) The letter vav, translated as "and," in the term "and like a wall," is
seemingly unnecessary;

c) Shortly afterwards, the Alter Rebbe speaks of "not standing like a wall,"
and does not mention "a column."

It is possible to explain that the Alter Rebbe is emphasizing that there
were two phases to the miracle. First, the waters stood like a column (a
collection and accumulation of water — see Rashi's commentary; this was the
only change. The water remained flowing; it was like water in a container
[except that there was no container]). Afterwards, it also stood like a wall
([i.e., it hardened;] it would no longer require a container to stand erect).

On this basis, we can appreciate the conceptual flow in Shaar HaYichud
VehaEmunah: Had not G-d continued the miracle, the water would have
flowed again (negating the flowing column; obviously, this would lead to the
negation of the following step), that it did not stand like a wall. (This is a
greater change and therefore there would be no doubt concerning it.)

The interpretation of this verse is relevant to the content of the chapter in
Shaar HaYichud VehaEmunah. For [it clarifies that] the miracle of the splitting
of the sea follows a step-by-step sequence that recognizes that natural order,
in contrast to the creation yesh meiayin, something from nothing, [which is
utterly transcendent].

29. [This was a miracle wrought by G-d;] it was not caused by the wind itself
(see the explanation of the Ramban in his commentary to Shmos 14:24). The
necessity for the wind was:

a) to leave room for the Egyptians to err, (as the Ramban writes); and

b) because the east (קדים) wind was the medium through which the
revelation of "He who preceded the world" (קדמונו של עולם), the level which
made possible the splitting of the sea (see the maamar entitled VaYolech
Havayah 5666, and other sources).

Nevertheless, from the explanation in Shaar HaYichud VehaEmunah (and
from the Rashbam and many other commentaries to the Torah), it appears
that the "strong east wind" caused the actual splitting of the sea. ([Saying
that the wind was unusually "strong"] resolves the question of the Ramban.)

The Alter Rebbe uses the concept: "If G-d would have stopped the wind
for a moment, the water would have returned and flowed downward as is its
natural pattern" as a proof that the same motif would be applicable with
regard to the creation of the heaven and earth. If G-d's creative power would
withdraw from the creation, the created beings would return to nothingness
[as they were before the creation]. For even if the splitting of the sea came
because of the wind, the wind brought about a change in the nature of the
water, causing it to stand like "a wall of stone."

water would have reverted to its original state. Hence, it is
not necessary for the verse:] "And towards morning, the sea
turned back to its power," to teach us this concept. Thus,
the question remains: What new concept does this verse
introduce?

For this reason, the *Midrash* interprets the verse as
meaning that the sea returned {not only to the strength it
possessed before it split (for that is not a new concept),
but} to the strength with which G-d endowed it at the
beginning of creation when He established the condition
with it to split for the Jewish people. This strength is
immeasurably greater than the strength the sea possesses
on its own accord (as will be explained in section V).

This condition was fulfilled when the sea split. Nevertheless, the verse states, "And... the sea turned back to its
power," because the strength with which the condition
endowed the sea was drawn down to it in a revealed
manner (not at the time when it split, but) when it reverted
to its original state (as explained in section VI). Through
the sea splitting, becoming as dry land, and then reverting
to sea, it came "to its power," "to its condition," to the
strength endowed it by the condition [G-d established].

IV. To resolve the above, it is necessary to understand why
it was necessary for G-d, at the time of the creation, to

According to this, it is (simply) understood why the Alter Rebbe adds the
phrases "like a wall," and "they did not stand like a wall." For from the
phrase "the water would have returned and flowed downward as is its natural
pattern" [would nullify] only the change that the water stood like a column
(see the previous note), [and this would not serve as a proof with regard to
the creation]. For the creation of the heaven and the earth made them a
[new] entity, and, nevertheless, if the power of the Creator would be withdrawn, the created beings would return to absolute nothingness.

{In that context, it is worthy to mention the debate concerning the Alter
Rebbe's words "this nature in the water" (whether the intent is the [new
nature] that it stood or its [established natural tendency] that it flowed
downward. See the letter touching on this subject printed in *Likkutei Biurim
LiTanya* (by R. Y. Korf). See also *Likkutei Sichos*, Vol. VII, p. 189, note 10.}

establish a condition with the sea to split for the Jewish people. On the surface, since G-d is the Master of the world, it is obvious that He has power and jurisdiction over the sea, and can cause it to split without having to establish a condition at the outset.[30]

The concept can be explained as follows: The creation was brought into being "for the sake of the Jewish people and for the sake of the Torah."[31] The intent is {not only that the world exists in order to give the Jews the opportunity to observe the Torah and its *mitzvos,* as one entity serves another, without having any [inner] connection to [the purpose] itself. Instead,} [the motive is that] the Jews, through their Divine service in the Torah and its *mitzvos* {and through carrying out [their worldly activities in a manner of] "Know Him in all your ways,"[32] and "All your deeds should be for the sake of heaven,"[33]} should make the world itself a dwelling for G-d.

---

30. In *Moreh Nevuchim,* Vol. II, ch. 29 (see the *Rambam's Commentary to the Mishnah, Avos* 5:6; Rabbeinu Bachaye on the above verse), it is explained that the reason for the condition is that "the world follows its natural pattern." And it is not appropriate "that nature change after creation or that a new will be aroused after the pattern was established."

{Firstly, the *Rambam* explains (*Moreh Nevuchim,* Vol. III, ch. 20) with regard to the concept "My thoughts are not your thoughts" (*Isaiah* 55:8), that even if miracles would be new developments arising at a later time, this would not be considered a change in G-d's will, Heaven forbid; see the commentary of the *Tosafos Yom Tov* to *Avos, loc. cit.* (Note the *Tosafos Yom Tov's* statements which explain that the *Rambam's* explanation — why it was necessary for G-d to establish a condition [with the created beings] — is [to explain questions others may raise] and does not reflect his own views.)}

Moreover, in order to resolve the question that miracles appear to reflect a change in G-d's will, it would be sufficient to implant the splitting of the sea in [the masterplan for] the creation. There would be no necessity that a condition be made with regard to the creation of the sea.

31. *Midrash Tanchuma* (Buber edition), *Parshas Bereishis,* secs. 3,5; *Rashi's* commentary to *Bereishis* 1:1. See also *Bereishis Rabbah* 1:1; *Vayikra Rabbah* 36:4.

32. *Mishlei* 3:6.

33. *Avos* 2:12. See *Likkutei Sichos,* Vol. III, pp. 907, 932, for an explanation of the advantages of [the Divine service implied by] "Know Him in all your ways," over [that implied by] "All your deeds should be for the sake of heaven."

The intent of making a dwelling for G-d is [making] a dwelling for His essence, like a dwelling for a mortal king, in which his entire essence is found in the dwelling.[34] Accordingly, [the existence of] the world itself has to be [structured] in a manner that enables it to also appreciate the aspect of G-dliness that transcends the G-dliness that was condensed according to the limits of the worlds. (This includes even the Divine power manifest in the creation of the worlds.)[35]

Therefore G-d established a condition with the sea, and with every other entity brought into being during the six days of creation,[36] that when the time came, they would change their nature for the sake of the Jewish people. Had He not established this condition,[37] i.e., had the creation itself not accepted the possibility for miracles and changes in the natural order, the result would be that the miracles and changes in the natural order that come about from the light which is (encompassing, *sovev,* and) above the worlds[38] would nullify the existence of the worlds.[39] Therefore G-d created the sea (— and all other created beings —) with the condition that it split for the Jewish people.

---

34. See the beginning of the series of *maamarim* entitled *Yom Tov Shel Rosh HaShanah 5666,* and other sources [where this concept is explained].
35. [Trans. Note — For even the G-dly power manifest in creation has limits.]
36. *Bereishis Rabbah* 5:5; see also *Zohar,* Vol. II, p. 198b.
37. See also the commentary of *Tosafos Yom Tov* cited above which states that the purpose of the conditions was to show that everything was created solely for the sake of the Jewish people.
38. See the *maamar* entitled *HaChodesh HaZeh 5666,* and other sources.
39. [Trans. Note: I.e., had G-d not made a condition with the creations, He still could have wrought miracles, but then the miracles would run contrary to the existence of the world. As the world exists within its own context, there would be no place for miracles. By establishing this condition, G-d enabled this dimension which by nature transcends the worlds to become an inner dimension of the world's being.

   Doing so, it changed the definition of the creation. For instead of the creation existing as an independent entity, something with an identity of its own, the creation itself took on the purpose identified with the Jewish people and the Torah. That mission became not only a fact that it was forced to accept because G-d is its Master, but the way it looked at itself, as it were.]

Torah Law states that when a condition is established beforehand in the proper manner, if the principal does not fulfill the condition, the matter is nullified entirely retroactively. Similarly, in this instance,[40] the manner in which the world was created was that [if it would not enable the Jews to observe the Torah and its *mitzvos*,] the existence of the creation would be nullified. It would be as if, at the outset, it had not been created. This was intended so that the existence of the sea itself [— and similarly, the entire creation —] should agree[41] to the change of the natural order.

V. Based on the above, it is understood that the condition which G-d stipulated with the sea (and similarly, with all the other created beings at the time of the creation), that it should split for the Jewish people, endowed it with far

---

40. A question could be raised. When a person makes a conditional agreement, the statement of the condition is merely a revelation that if the condition is not fulfilled, the matter will not be concluded from the outset. With regard to the creation of heaven and earth, since they were already created, and until this moment, they actually existed, by contrast, it is seemingly difficult to understand how their existence could be nullified retroactively.

This question is, however, not justified. For when a person establishes a condition, the condition is not merely a clarification of the matter. Instead, the nullification of the condition is the factor which causes the matter to be nullified (see *Rambam, Mishneh Torah, Hilchos Geirushin* 8:22 and the gloss of the *Maggid Mishnah*).

Similar concepts apply when "a wise man revokes a vow from the outset." The essential effect of his revocation is future-oriented, for until the time [of his revocation], the article was forbidden. Nevertheless, [theoretically,] the revocation of the wise man nullifies the vow from its inception, and it is as if the article had never been forbidden (the gloss of Rabbeinu Asher to *Nedarim*, 52b).

41. See *Likkutei Sichos*, Vol. V, p. 11, note 40, with regard to the transformation of the land of the gentiles to *Eretz Yisrael*, which emphasizes that it is important that the gentiles also agree to this. See also *Toras Shalom*, p. 70, and notes, which state that "The sparks from the world of *Tohu* should also agree [to their refinement]."

To cite [a related matter]: The nullification of a false deity must be performed by a gentile, [not a Jew] (*Avodah Zarah* 52b). And [in a larger sense,] any entity that considers itself as separate, it is apart and a false divinity (*Tanya*, ch. 22).

greater power than it possessed by virtue of its creation itself (as it would have existed without the condition).

When an entity exists for a specific time, and then its existence ceases, even during the time it existed, its existence is weak.[42] Indeed, this weakness is the reason why afterwards, the entity ceases to exist.[43]

Therefore one may conclude that the world (as it exists in its own right, by virtue of its being brought into being by the Ten Utterances of Creation) does not possess true power. For it will exist for only six thousand years and then it will cease.[44]

---

42. For this reason, rivers which dry up once within a seven-year period* are not acceptable to be used for waters for the ashes of the *parah adumah* (the red heifer). For their waters are not considered as "living waters," but as "false waters" (*Parah* 8:9).

---

* Rivers which dry up once in a longer period, by contrast, are not considered as "false waters" (*Rambam, Mishneh Torah, Hilchos Parah* 6:12; see also the commentary of the *Tosafos Yom Tov* to the above *Mishnah*).

This is not considered a contradiction to the concept stated above: that if an existence will cease, it is not a genuine entity. Since the entire existence of our world is "false," (for it exists only for 6000 years,) we are forced to say that the concept of "living waters" [is relative], reflecting the "life" of the creation itself. Since every seven-year cycle is an independent interval (for this reason, the commentaries explain, the land is declared ownerless once in seven years), when an entity ceases to exist over a duration of time longer than seven years, it is not considered as "false" when compared to the pattern prevalent within our world.

(This also explains the view (espoused by Rav Ovadiah of Bartenura, Rabbeinu Shimon, and Rabbeinu Asher) that a river is not considered "false" if it ceases to flow only once in a *Yovel* [a 50-year cycle]. For a *Yovel* is considered as being "forever," as *Kiddushin* 15a and *Rashi* interpret *Shmos* 21:6: "He shall serve him forever."

43. See the *Sefer HaChakirah* by the *Tzemach Tzedek*, p. 4a, p. 104a ff., the second *maamar* entitled *Ein Aroch 5694* (*Sefer HaMaamarim 5711*), sec. 30; the *maamar* entitled *Tiku 5707, et al.*

44. See the *maamarim* entitled *HaUmnam Yeshav 5643*, ch. 4; *Kol HaShoneh Halachos 5667*; *Tiku 5694* (*Sefer HaMaamarim 5711*), et al.

In other sources, a different explanation is offered: That the entities of the heaven and the earth are as strong today as they were on the day that they were created, and it is only because of G-d's will that they will cease to exist after the 6000 years of creation (*Sefer HaChakirah* 3b, 101b ff., the *maamarim* entitled *Ein Aroch* and *Tiku, loc. cit.*).

Because of the condition that G-d established with it at the time of its Creation, [the world] receives greater and more encompassing strength. The fact that He created the world with the condition "that it carry out the will of the righteous even though it is against its nature" shows that although G-d created the world "for the sake of the Jewish people," that intent is an inner dimension of the world itself.

{For if the concept that the world was created "for the sake of the Jewish people" was that one entity serve another although it has no connection to it, it would not be appropriate to say that the creation was brought into being so that the world would go against its nature.}

The Jews are "the sprouting of [G-d's] planting, the work of [His] hands."[45] Therefore they are eternal, an entity of [G-d's] thought[46] which is the source and the reason (for the existence of) His speech, [the medium through which the world was brought into being]. By making "the fulfillment of the will of the righteous" [a condition] within the existence of the creation itself, G-d introduced a dimension

---

[Even according to this explanation, however, there is a dimension of entropy within the creation. For] the infinite power that is invested in the creation (which endows them with eternality, that their strength will remain [constant], as on the day of their creation) is beyond their existence and does not become one with them {the maamar entitled *Tzohar Taaseh 5673* (in the series of maamarim entitled *BeShaah SheHikdimu 5672*); see also *Likkutei Sichos,* Vol. V, p. 98, note 21}.

{[The rationale is] that it is impossible that an unlimited power can enclothe itself in a limited entity, as the *Rambam* writes (*Moreh Nevuchim,* Vol. II, Introduction 12): "For every power that is found expressing itself within a body is limited, for the material entity is limited."}

And as the entity exists in its own right (i.e., as the creations are brought into being from the Ten Utterances of Creation that enclothe themselves within them), they are breaking down, [becoming simplified], as explained in *Likkutei Sichos, loc. cit.*

45. *Yeshayahu* 60:21. Thus *Sanhedrin* 10:1 [cites this verse as the prooftext for the teaching that all Jews will receive a portion of the World to Come, the world which is eternal and not subject to the vicissitudes of time].

46. For "Israel arose in His thought" (*Bereishis Rabbah* 1:1).

of eternality into them which transcends their own existence.[47]

VI. On this basis, we can appreciate the interpretation
offered by the *Midrash* to the verse: "And towards morning,
the sea turned back to its power," "as per the condition
established with it at the outset." While the sea was split,
one could think that the miracle (changed and) nullified the
sea's previous existence,[48] and thus the strength with which
the fulfillment of the condition endowed the sea was not
revealed.

When, however, the sea "turned back" — {and "turned
back to its power," which as implied by its simple meaning
is that its nature did not change (as stated in section I) and
yet, its own existence left room for doing G-d's will against
its nature} [a change was brought about]. Through the
fulfillment of the condition, the sea attained its strength,
i.e., a far greater dimension of strength than it possess by
virtue of its own existence.

Adapted from Sichos Shabbos Parshas Beshallach, 5729

---

47. The miraculous pattern of conduct [within the world] stems from the light
which is *Sovev Kol Almim,* the light which encompasses and transcends the
worlds, as stated in sec. V. Thus because of the light of *Sovev Kol Almim,* [it
appears that] there is a dimension of eternality within the creation itself even
without G-d's having established a condition with it (see note 43).

It is possible to explain [the manner in which the condition G-d established with the world augments its existence as follows]: Since the creations
were brought into being with the intent that they "carry out the will of the
righteous even though it is against their nature," this intent shares a connection to the existence of the created beings themselves.

{From one point, this dimension is more transcendent than the infinite
power that maintains the constancy of the natural order, as reflected by the
fact that [these miracles] bring about a disruption of the natural order (see
the *maamar* entitled *HaChodesh HaZeh,* 5666). Nevertheless, since it involves a
condition according to which the creation was brought into being, [it relates
to the inner dimension of the creation].

To use wording (borrowed from the *Rambam, Moreh Nevuchim, loc. cit.*), the
power which maintains the existence of a limited creation for an unlimited
time cannot enclothe itself within the creation itself. The power which makes
water stand as a wall, [i.e., performs miracles,] by contrast, [relates to the
inner dimension of the created being].}

48. See the commentary of the *Or HaChayim* cited above.

Parshas Yisro

Likkutei Sichos, Vol. VI, p. 107ff.

I.   "And on the third day, when it was morning, there were sounds (קולות) and lightning; and there was a heavy cloud on the mountain. And the sound (קול) of the *shofar* [resounded] very powerfully... And the sound (קול) of the *shofar* continued.... And G-d answered him in a [loud] voice (קול)."[1]

This verse mentions five קולות, sounds or voices.[2] Commenting on this, the *Talmud* states:[3] A person who brings joy to a bridegroom will acquire the Torah, for the Torah was given with five קולות, and there are five קולות mentioned with regard to a bridegroom: "the voice (קול) of joy, the voice (קול) of happiness, the voice (קול) of a groom and the voice (קול) of a bride, and a voice (קול) stating: 'Give thanks to the G-d of Hosts.'"[4]

The reason a person who brings joy to a bridegroom will acquire the Torah is that there is an inner connection between the fundamental nature of these two entities.[5] (It is not appropriate to say that a person who brings joy to a bridegroom should acquire the Torah merely because the

---

1. *Shmos* 19:16-19,

2. [I.e., the word קול is mentioned three times, and קולות, the plural form, i.e., at least two, is mentioned once.]

3. *Berachos* 6b.

4. *Yirmeyahu* 33:11.

5. See the *Chidushei Aggados* of the *Maharsha* to *Berachos*, loc. cit., which [explains the connection between the Torah and a bridegroom as follows: The Torah] was given on the day of [G-d's] rejoicing and the day of His marriage with the Jewish people.

same number of קולות are mentioned in both contexts without there being an inner connection between the two subjects. On the contrary,) the reason the same number of קולות are mentioned with regard to both the Torah and a bridegroom is that there is an inner connection between them.

Thus the Alter Rebbe explains[6] that the reason a person who brings joy to a bridegroom acquires the Torah is based on the principle "measure for measure."[7] The Torah itself (is called a bridegroom, because) the influence that it conveys to the Jewish people resembles the influence conveyed by a bridegroom to his bride.

The reason the *Talmud* [does not mention the thematic connection, and instead] focuses on the five קולות mentioned in connection with the giving of the Torah (even though on the surface, it appears to be merely an external consequence) is that the number of קולות mentioned in connection with the Torah and a bridegroom expresses the inner connection[8] that reflects the essence of both the Torah and a bridegroom.

The Torah was given with five קולות, the same number of קולות mentioned with regard to a bridegroom, (not only because both the Torah and a bridegroom convey influence, for that is an obvious fact that does not require any proof, but also) because [they both convey the same type of influence]. For the influence the Torah conveys to the Jewish

---

6. *Likkutei Torah, Devarim*, p. 94a.
7. *Sanhedrin* 90a.
8. See *Likkutei Sichos*, Vol. I, p. 57, which explains our Sages' statement (*Pirkei d'R. Eliezer*, ch. 32): "ten blessings... corresponding to the Ten Utterances of Creation." The connection between the blessings and the utterances stems from their essential nature (and therefore, the numbers associated with them are the same). {Similar concepts apply with regard to many statements of our Sages which emphasize a numerical connection between two subjects.}

  [One might ask: If so, the order should be reversed, and the emphasis should be placed on the utterances, for they are the source for the blessing.] Nevertheless, the blessings are mentioned first, because in certain matters, our pattern of deduction works from the end result to the source, as explained at length in that source.

people cannot be compared to a teacher's conveying a concept to a student, but instead resembles the inner, lofty influence that a bridegroom conveys to his bride, as will be explained.

All concepts in Torah are precise and serve as a lesson. Similarly, the fact that the *Talmud* focuses on the number of קולות mentioned in connection with the Torah and a bridegroom (and not merely that they share the same number of קולות) indicates that the number five also provides a lesson for us in this context.

II. The unique quality associated with the Torah that is expressed by the mention of five[9] קולות (and which expresses the special connection between the Torah and a bridegroom) can be understood by prefacing the explanation of the concept of a קול.

A קול draws down and reveals an entity's quality; something that was previously hidden is revealed.[10] For example, a human being's voice reveals his intellect or his emotions.

Moreover, a person's voice reflects and parallels the subject that it reveals. {For example, the tone of voice that expresses a command — a high and stern pitch — is different from the tone of voice which communicates an intellectual concept, as it is written:[11] "The words of the wise are heard[12] gently."[13]}

---

9. See the *maamar* of the Alter Rebbe entitled *Lahavin Inyan Chamishah Kolos* (*Maamarei Admur HaZakein 5565*, Vol. I, p. 43) and several explanations of the verse from the *Tzemach Tzedek* in *Or HaTorah* in the *maamar* entitled *VeChol HaAm Roi'im* (p. 958ff.).

10. See *Torah Or*, p. 74c, *Likkutei Torah, Bamidbar* 29a ff.
    In the texts of Jewish philosophy and *Kabbalah*, the concept of five קולות is discussed by the *Rambam* in *Moreh Nevuchim*, Vol. II, ch. 33 and the *Avodas HaKodesh* (who questions the *Rambam's* statements,) Vol. IV, ch. 31. See also the *maamar* in *Or HaTorah* from the *Tzemach Tzedek* cited above.

11. *Koheles* 9:17.

12. See the *maamarim* entitled *Shoftim*, 5672, and *Tiku*, 5707, sec. 3.

13. Similarly, we find *Shmos* 32:18 speaking of "a voice resounding with strength,... a voice resounding with weakness... a voice of distress."

Similarly, in the spiritual realms,[14] there are different
קולות, modes of expression, each one distinguished from the
other. The distinction between them reflects the difference
in the objective each קול is intended to accomplish.

From this, we can appreciate that the fact that the Torah
was given with five different קולות, modes of expression,
indicates that there are five different dimensions, one
higher than the other,[15] each one being drawn down
through one of the five types of קולות.

This also explains the unique dimension of the Torah —
that it was given with five voices. As is well known,[16] the
entire spiritual cosmos is divided into four types of worlds
(which parallel the four forms of earthly existence: inanimate objects, plants, animals, and humans[17]). Moreover,
these four different levels are reflected, not only in the
worlds which are brought into being, but also in G-d's name
Havayah (ה-ו-ה-י), [18] the active agent which brings the worlds
into existence. For this name contains the four letters that
serve as the source for the four worlds[19] (and within each
world, for the four forms of existence: inanimate objects,
plants, animals, and humans, in that world[20]).

---

14. See the commentaries to *Tehillim* 29:3ff., and our Sages' interpretation of
those verses.

15. Based on the above, we can resolve the differences between this statement of
our Sages mentioning five voices and other statements of our Sages (*Shmos
Rabbah,* 28:6, the commentary of *Ramban*) which mention seven voices [asso-
ciated with the giving of the Torah]. For all seven voices mentioned are
associated with one level, our [seven] emotional attributes. See also the
commentary of the *Rikanti.*

16. [In addition to the sources in *Kabbalah* and *Chassidus,*] see also *Moreh
Nevuchim,* Vol. II, ch. 10.

17. See the *maamarim* entitled *Chavivin Yisrael,* 5696, and *Azehu Chacham,* 5702,
sec. V, *et al,* [where these concepts are explained] at length.

18. Indeed, as explained in *Tanya, Shaar HaYichud VehaEmunah,* ch. 4, the name
Havayah relates to the term *mehaveh,* bringing into existence.

19. *Likkutei Torah, Bamidbar* 95a, *et al.*

20. *Tanya,* ch. 38 (p. 50b). See also *Torah Or* 3c ff., and *Toras Chayim,* p. 19c ff.,
which explain the connection between the four forms of existence: inanimate
objects, plants, animals, and humans, and the four letters of the name
Havayah.

Since G-d "looked into the Torah and created the world,"[21] it follows that the same pattern that applies to the life-energy vested in the worlds exists in the Torah. Indeed, [the order is reversed, the pattern begins in the Torah, and from] the Torah is drawn down [into the world]. And thus the Torah also contains the four levels ([that reflect the four letters] of the name *Havayah*.

Based on the above, we can understand the uniqueness of the fact that the Torah was given with five voices,[22] i.e., together with the four levels that stem from the name *Havayah* and which are reflected in the spiritual cosmos, the Torah contains a fifth dimension which transcends the name *Havayah* (even the *Yud* of the name *Havayah*).

This concept is alluded to [in the first of the Ten Commandments] which begins (reflecting an order of descent from Above): *Anochi Havayah E-lokecha* ("I am *Havayah*, your G-d"). *Anochi* refers to "[G-d] as [He] is [for Himself], who cannot at all be defined by a name, nor alluded to in a letter, or even in a point of a letter."[23] *Havayah* [refers to the four levels of the spiritual cosmos as above]. And *E-lokecha* means "your strength[24] and your life-energy.[25] All five dimensions of the Torah, even the level that transcends the name *Havayah*, were endowed to [the Jews as they live in] this physical world. This represents the uniqueness of the Torah having been given with five voices.

III. We have no way of comprehending spiritual concepts as they exist on their own level. The only way we can [appreciate these concepts] is through the material entities that have their source in them. Through [understanding these material entities, and then through abstraction and deduc-

21. *Zohar*, Vol. II, p. 161a,b.
22. Note a similar concept explained in *Or HaTorah*, Yisro, pp. 961-962.
23. *Likkutei Torah*, Bamidbar 80b; see *Zohar*, Vol. III, p. 257b.
24. *Tur* and *Shulchan Aruch* (*Orach Chayim* 5:1).
25. See *Torah Or*, Parshas Yisro, p. 67b.

tion,] we can develop some tentative assumptions with regard to the spiritual entities which are their source.[26]

Thus we can develop some conception of what is meant by the four letters of the name *Havayah* {and thus the awesome uniqueness of the Torah which was given with five voices, transcending the name *Havayah* as explained above} by explaining the four forms of existence — inanimate objects, plants, animals, and humans — that exist in our world. For they "parallel the four letters of the name *Havayah* and receive influence from them."[27]

[To explain:] The difference between inanimate matter and plants is that with regard to inanimate matter, we see only the actual physical entity; it does not express life at all. Although it possesses a "soul," i.e., a source of spiritual, life-energy,[28] [there is no outward manifestation of that spiritual energy]. With regard to plants, by contrast, it is obvious that they contain spiritual life-energy which cannot be perceived by our five senses.

(In a certain way,) this distinction is much greater than the distinctions between plants and animals or humans.[29] For all of these entities share a common denominator; their spiritual vitality is revealed. (The difference between them involves merely the extent and the nature of that revelation, as will be explained.) With regard to inanimate matter,

---

26. See *Sefer HaSichos 5702*, p. 76ff., *Sefer HaSichos 5703*, p. 148ff.; see also note 7.
27. *Tanya*, ch. 38.
28. See *Tanya, Shaar HaYichud VehaEmunah*, ch. 1. See the explanation of all the above in the end of the text *Etz Chayim*. [These texts explain how every entity which exists is maintained by the G-dly energy that is enclothed within it.]
29. Similar concepts apply with regard to the four spiritual worlds: *Atzilus, Beriah Yetzirah*, and *Asiyah* (which parallel the four forms of existence: inanimate objects, plants, animals, and humans). The phrase (*Yeshayahu* 43:7): "I even made it" is interpreted as a reference to the world of *Asiyah*. (That phrase contains the term "even," indicating an interruption.) For deed represents a separate entity [unlike speech and thought where there is still some connection with the thinker or the speaker]. See *Likkutei Torah*, the beginning of *Parshas Balak, et al.*

however, there is no revelation of the spiritual energy it contains.

Nevertheless, on the whole, the plant kingdom can be considered closer to inanimate matter than to animals or humans.[30] Indeed, when the four forms of existence — inanimate objects, plants, animals, and humans — are divided into two categories: those which are predominantly associated with the body and those which are predominantly associated with the soul, the plant kingdom, together with inanimate matter, are placed in the category of the body. Animals and humans, by contrast, are placed in the category of soul.[31] Indeed, the very Hebrew name for the plant kingdom, *tzomei'ach*, which means "growing," is a marked contrast from the name for the animal kingdom, *chai*, which means "living." The distinction between the two is reflected in the fact that before the flood, mankind was allowed to eat only plant-life and was not allowed to eat animals.[32]

The reason for this difference can be explained as follows. [There are two qualities which distinguish the life-energy of] an animal:

a) The life-energy is associated with a soul, [a conscious entity with a sensation of self]. For this reason, an animal

---

30. A parallel is found with regard to the distinctions between the four spiritual worlds, *Atzilus, Beriah, Yetzirah, and Asiyah*. See note 73.

31. See *Tanya, loc. cit.,* (p. 51a). See also the Rebbe Rashab's notes to *Tanya* (*Kitzurim VeHaaros LiTanya*, p. 115): "[The text] does not say "the soul of an inanimate object or a plant. That term is used only with regard to humans and animals."

32. See *Sanhedrin* 59b (cited in *Rashi's* commentary to *Bereishis* 9:3). See also *Sanhedrin* 57a.

   The distinction between plants and animals is also relevant in the present age. There is a prohibition that forbids eating *ever min hachai*, a limb from a living animal, while there is no such prohibition with regard to eating plant-life that is still connected to its source of nurture.

possesses the power of will[33] (which expresses the soul[34]); and

b) Because the body and the soul are unified,[35] the body is naturally affected by the will of the soul [and carries out its desires][36] to the extent that the definition [of the body changes].[37] [It does] not [see itself as] matter, but is [identified with] the soul.[38]

---

33. See *Rambam, Mishneh Torah, Hilchos Yesodei HaTorah* 3:11 and the *Peirush* [which describe the nature of inanimate matter].

34. This is reflected in the interpretation of *Yirmeyahu* 15:1 אין נפשי אל העם הזה. *Rashi* interprets נפשי (which would ordinarily be interpreted as "my soul") as "my desire."* See also *Kitzurim VeHaaros LiTanya, loc. cit.*, which states: "Inanimate matter and plants which do not possess will and feeling... are not called 'a soul.'"

---

* This concept is quoted in *Torah Or*, p. 36b, *Kitzurim VeHaaros, loc. cit.*, and other places in *Chassidus*. See the note on p. 227 of *Sefer HaMaamarim 5709*, which explains why this verse is frequently cited as a proof of this concept.

35. See *Torah Or*, p. 13a, *et al.*

36. "Without the necessity for a command or statement" (*Tanya*, ch. 23).

37. This reflects the difference between the *bittul* of the body to the soul and the *bittul* of a chariot to its driver. Since the chariot is a separate entity, distinct from the driver (although nullified to him), it must be directed by the driver. Since the limbs of the body, by contrast, are unified with the soul, they follow the will of the soul as a matter of course (the *maamar* entitled *Kol Machlokes*, 5671).

38. As is well known (see the *maamar* entitled *Ki Imcha*, 5700, ch. 2), the relationship of the body to the soul can be defined as *mahus* and *metzius*.

[Trans. Note: The Hebrew term *mahus* (מהות) is derived from the two words *ma hu* (מה הוא) which mean: "What it is." An entity's *mahus* is its fundamental identity, what that entity is. *Metzius* means "existence," the entity's outward existence.

The soul is the *mahus* of the body. In other words, the body does not see itself as a separate entity in which the soul is lodged. Instead, it is identified with the soul to the extent that it defines itself in terms of the soul. The soul is its "I." When a person stubs his toe, he does not see his toe as a separate entity from himself; it is he himself who feels the pain. His body exists to manifest his soul.]

Thus [our Sages rule] that "a living entity carries itself,"* and indeed, does not feel itself as separate [from its life-energy] (the *maamar* entitled *Yecheinu MiYomi'im*, 5701, ch. 2).

---

* *Shabbos* 94a. Although the Sages differ and rule (and their opinion is accepted as *halachah, Shulchan Aruch HaRav* 308:80) that a person who transfers an animal or a beast to the public domain is liable [for the violation of the *Shabbos* laws, they do not object to the theoretical basis of the concept. Instead, their

In contrast, not only does the life-energy of a plant not make a change in the nature of its body, but the life-energy is itself bodily oriented. For its entire purpose is to make the body grow and become larger.

IV. Another distinction between a plant and an animal is that the life-energy (and growth) of a plant is dependent on the fact that it is rooted in a specific place. (If it is uprooted from that place, it will no longer [be alive or] grow. The life-energy of an animal, in contrast, is not limited to any specific place.[39]

The reason for this distinction is that a material entity is defined by place. Thus, since the life-energy of a plant is [subordinate to] its body, it is limited to a specific place. In contrast, an animal's life-energy is spiritual in nature and therefore it is not as bound by the limitations of place.

As mentioned above, although the two forms of existence — inanimate matter and plants — both belong to the same category, i.e., the body, from a certain perspective, the difference between them is greater than the difference between a plant and an animal (see section III). Similarly (and indeed, to a greater extent), there is a distinction between the two forms of existence which are identified with the soul, animals and humans. For humans are entirely distinct from animals: humans are the chosen creations and all the other created beings (including animals) were created for the sake of serving humans.[40]

[As mentioned,] the point that distinguishes inanimate matter from other forms of existence (including plants) is

---

position stems from the fact that an animal] makes itself difficult to hold and tries to slip from the holder's grasp. [Their position] does not reflect on [the relationship between the animal's body and] its soul.

39. We find that there is a living entity called *Adnei HaSadeh* (*Kilayim* 8:5) which also has limitations. See *Etz Chayim, Shaar* 42, which considers that entity as an intermediary between a plant and an animal.

40. As our Sages state (at the conclusion of tractate *Kiddushin*): "They (fowls and animals) were created solely to serve me."

that with regard to inanimate matter, all that is perceived is
the material form (as stated above). Similarly with regard to
the other extreme, the point which distinguishes mankind
from the other created beings (even from animals) is that it
is within mankind that the true concept of soul and spirituality is expressed.

VI. The true description of spirituality is that it is not
bounded by any particular boundary, [that its existence is
higher] than what can be perceived, even by powers which
are higher than the five senses that can appreciate a physical
entity. A spiritual entity also has a specific definition which
delineates its existence and separates it from another spiritual entity.[41] Nevertheless, because of its spiritual nature
(and its refinement), there is a sensation of *peshitus*[42]
(simplicity[43]) within it which is above comprehension.[44]

41. See the *Rambam, Mishneh Torah, Hilchos Yesodei HaTorah* 2:5-7.
42. See the *maamar* entitled *Lulav ViAravah*, 5659, which explains that the fundamental definition of the qualities of the soul comes about because of their
enclothment within the limbs of the body. We are compelled to say that
there exists a definition of these qualities within the soul itself.(For even as
the soul exists in the spiritual worlds, it possesses [these qualities, for] it
comprehends [spiritual concepts] and expresses the emotions [of love and
fear]. Nevertheless

> In truth, it is a wondrous matter for us and we really do not know at all
> how it is possible for there to be a definition of powers [as the soul exists
> in the spiritual realms] and how [these powers] exist. For the possibility
> that a definition of powers should exist within a spiritual entity which is
> above a material form and garment is not understandable to us at all. [We
> cannot comprehend] how it is possible that there could be a definition of
> powers [in a spiritual entity] and how that definition would be expressed.
> As explained in the note 44, even the definition of the powers as they
> exist after being enclothed in the body is not a strict definition.

43. [Trans. Note: I.e., an integral oneness that stems from a lack of definition.
Material entities are defined by the three dimensions: length, width, and
height. Even though spiritual entities are not defined by such limits, they,
too, have their definitions. And yet, over and above these definitions, there is
a fundamental oneness that characterizes all spiritual entities.]
44. Note the letter of the Previous Rebbe (printed at the conclusion of *Kuntres
HaAvodah*, p. 54) which [mentions three types of love and] states:

> A spiritual entity is not confined by a stone barrier... by the appearances of
> different colors... or the varying flavors of sweetness.... Therefore, within

The simplicity which can be perceived in spiritual entities has several manifestations. Among them:

a) A spiritual entity does not contradict another entity.[45]
We see this point reflected with regard to refined, abstract
ideas. The more refined and abstract they are, the less they
contradict each other.[46]

b) Its spiritual nature causes it to seek to rise above
itself. (We see this quality manifest in the [reflections of]
spirituality [that exist] within [our] material [world]. For
example, fire is the most refined of the four fundamental
elements.[47] Because of this spiritual quality, its nature[48] is to

---

all three types of love, there will be found offshoots that resemble one
another and are similar to one another.

On the surface, the distinctions between the three forms of love mentioned are spiritual; how then does the fact that a spiritual entity is not
bound by the limitations of substance and matter demonstrate that within
the three types of love, there are offshoots that resemble each other? [For
even though these types of love are not bound by material definitions, they
are seemingly bound by spiritual definitions, and each one has a nature of its
own.]

[The resolution of this question is that] because of the simplicity which
characterizes spiritual existence, even though each one of the three types of
love is defined by its own character, we are nevertheless forced to say that it
includes within itself dimensions of the other types of love. Further clarification of the matter is, however, still required.

45. We find that several spiritual entities can be found in the same place {see
     Likkutei Torah, Nitzavim, p. 49a; the maamar entitled Ki Cheilek, 5694 (Sefer
     HaMaamarim 5711), ch. 10; Kuntres Limud HaChassidus, ch. 17ff.}. Neverthe-
     less, this does not prove the above concept fully, because such an
     interrelation is not (reflective of their essential nature, but merely) [a result
     of] their being in the same place. [The fundamental point is, however,] that
     even the essential nature of [a spiritual entity] is not circumscribed and
     defined in a complete manner, as explained in the previous note.

46. See the maamar entitled Shelach, 5672.

47. Of the four elements: fire, air, water, and earth, it is fire which is comparable
     to humans (in the four types of existence] {Toras Chayim, Bereishis, p. 19c. See
     the maamar entitled Ner Chanukah, 5666 (the series of maamarim entitled Yom
     Tov Shel Rosh HaShanah, 5666, p. 115) which explains that the statements in
     Tanya, ch. 19, follow the opinion of the Etz Chayim, Shaar Derushei Abiyah, ch.
     1} and to Atzilus [in the four worlds] (Likkutei Torah, Shir HaShirim, p. 4d; Or
     HaTorah, Yisro, p. 826; the maamarim entitled Zeh HaYom, 5660, and Vihar
     Sinai, 5662).

48. See also Bamidbar Rabbah 14:12, Tanya, loc. cit.

ascend upward.[49]) For its true quality[50] is not to remain [limited] within its particular identity, but to rise above itself and become included in its source in the higher realms.

VII. The above also explains why humans reflect the true definition of soul and spirituality, because the advantage of humans over animals is the power of intellect[51] which possesses both of the above-mentioned qualities:

a) [A person's] intellect is not confined by the nature of his emotional make-up. Since a person possesses an intel-

---

Based on the above statements — that fire's tendency to rise stems from its spiritual quality — it is possible to explain the Alter Rebbe's statement in *Tanya* that "the light of the fire possesses a natural desire" [i.e., his emphasis is on "the light of the fire" and not merely fire]. For although even the material dimension of fire is spiritual (when compared to [the other three elements:] air, water, and earth), the spiritual dimension within it cannot be compared to the spiritual dimension in the *light* of the fire. Therefore, when the Alter Rebbe speaks of "the desire to separate from its wick and cling to its source," he is referring (primarily) to the *light* of the fire.

49. See the *maamar* entitled *Kivod Malchuscha*, 5661.

50. See the above *maamar* which explains that the statement in *Tanya*, that fire possesses a natural desire to rise upward, indicates that this tendency to rise upward is {not (an incremental dimension of its being) [stemming] from its appreciation of the higher quality of its source. Instead, because of} its essential spiritual quality (i.e., its lack of [defined] existence), it desires to rise above its existence entirely.

There is a question whether this explanation can be corroborated with [the explanation often given for fire's tendency to rise,] that each entity is drawn to its source. Hence earth descends downward, and fire rises, [because of its higher source]. It is possible to explain that [the latter explanation refers to] the material dimension [of fire], while [the previous explanation] refers to its light.

51. See *Rambam, Hilchos Yesodei HaTorah*, 4:8, [which states that the power of knowledge is the unique dimension of soul granted to man]; see also the *maamar* entitled *Vayavo Amalek*, 5709 (based on the *Rambam's* Introduction to his *Commentary to the Mishnah*), et al. This view is also reflected in *Tanya*, ch. 38 (p. 51a).

See sec. X which [takes a somewhat different tact and] explains that the fundamental advantage that man possesses (which distinguishes him from the animals) is the source for his power of speech. Therefore when referring to man, our Sages called him *midaber*, a speaker. See *Torah Or*, p. 3d [which appears to fuse both these views saying]: "In humans, in addition to all the above, there is the intellectual soul, the soul which speaks."

lectual capacity,[52] he is not forced to retain the fundamental tendencies to which he has an inherent inclination.[53] (While other created beings, by contrast, cannot change their natures,) man has free choice to embrace any path he desires [to follow].[54]

This is also the reason why a person includes within himself all the other forms of existence contained within creation, (for which reason, he is called[55] "a world in microcosm.") For he is not confined by any limitations.[56]

---

52. *Likkutei Torah, Vayikra,* p. 38b, states that man's power of choice stems from the fact that the *Or Ein Sof,* (G-d's infinite light) {which transcends the intellectual faculties of *Chabad,* see *ibid.:a*} rests within man.

   [Nevertheless, this does not represent a contradiction.] For as explained in that source, the *Or Ein Sof* rests in the realm of *Tikkun.* It is understood that this relates to the quality of intellect (or enclothes itself in intellect), for the gestalt of *Tikkun* is fundamentally determined by the intellect. See also the *Rambam, Mishneh Torah, Hilchos Teshuvah* 5:1 (quoted in *Likkutei Torah, loc. cit.*) which describes [man's power of choice] [as follows]: "He can, on his own initiative, with his knowledge... do anything that he desires." See also *Tanya, loc. cit.,* which [describes man as possessing] intellect and choice.

   See also *Toras Chayim, Toldos,* p. 14b ff.; and the *maamar* entitled *Min HaMeitzar,* 5660 and the *maamar* which follows it.

53. See ch. 8 of the *Rambam's Shemoneh Perakim* (the *Rambam's Commentary to the Mishnah,* Introduction to tractate *Avos,* ch. 8); the gloss of the *Lechem Mishneh* to *Hilchos Teshuvah,* 5:4; *Toras Chayim, loc. cit.,* p. 14a; *Shaar HaBechirah* of the Mitteler Rebbe, ch. 7.

54. It is possible to see that the reason [for this distinction] is that in animals, the character tendencies are firmly established, while with regard to man, he is merely (as the *Rambam* states) fit for a positive or negative quality. [This is, however, not a sufficient explanation, because:]

   a) Even with regard to a human being, being "fit" [for a quality] means that he has an inclination toward it {to the extent that because of this inclination, he can be labeled as "wicked," as *Tehillim* 58:4 states: "The wicked are estranged from the womb."}. And thus, a person requires unique power to be able to choose to act contrary to this inherent tendency;

   b) The reason why a person's tendencies are not firmly established is that {his source is from the level of (Sublime Wisdom) which is above any definite characteristic (as explained in *Toras Chayim, loc. cit.*)}. And this level is also the source for man's power of choice.

55. See *Bereishis Rabbah,* chs. 8, 12; *Koheles Rabbah,* ch. 1; *Avos d'R. Nosan,* ch. 31, where the concept is explained at length.

56. See *Likkutei Torah, Vayikra,* p. 37c ff., *et al.*

b) The tendency of intellect is to (withdraw from itself[57] and) approach a plane higher than itself. In this, there is also a fundamental difference between a human being (whose character is defined by intellect) and an animal (whose character is defined by emotions). For "the spirit of man ascends upward, and the spirit of an animal descends downward,"[58] i.e., an animal has a tendency for material things, while a person seeks to rise above himself.

VIII. From the fact that a person is "a world in microcosm" (as explained in section VII), it can be understood that the four forms of existence that are found in the world in macrocosm also [have parallels] that are apparent[59] in man's "world in microcosm," not only in his body, but also within his soul. As is explained within *Chassidus*,[60] the letters [within our soul, see the definition which follows] represent the quality of inanimate matter within the soul. Emotions parallel plant life, intellect, animals, and the source for the power of speech, humanity.

The concept can be explained as follows: The Hebrew word for letters, אותיות, (relates to the word אתא[61] as in the phrase[62] אתא בוקר, "morning is coming") and is identified with manifestation and revelation. The letters [within our souls] are distinguished from the other powers of the soul in that the other powers affect the [character of the person

---

57. [Trans. Note: The concept of withdrawal refers to the mind's desire to ascend to a higher plane. Instead of nurturing its present framework of existence, it seeks to ascend to a higher plane.]

58. *Koheles* 3:21. Note the *maamar* entitled *Shechorah Ani*, 5702, which states: "An animal has never seen the heavens and does not know of the fact that the heavens exist."

59. While with regard to animals, plants and inanimate objects, [by contrast, these four qualities are not overtly apparent]. See the *maamar* entitled *Lehavin Inyan... HaNekudim, Maamarei Admur HaZakein 5568*, Vol. I, p. 111.

60. *Torah Or*, p. 4a ff.; *Likkutei Torah, Bamidbar*, p. 58a; *Toras Chayim Bereishis* p. 19d ff.; the *maamarim* entitled *Chavivin Yisrael*, 5696, and *Eizahu Chacham*, 5702, ch. 5.

61. See *Torah Or*, p. 42b, *et al.*

62. *Yeshayahu* 21:12.

himself], (for example, emotions describe an individual's personality, whether he is a generous person or a stern individual).[63] Letters, by contrast, are merely mediums through which the person's powers become manifest and expressed. They themselves do not affect the person himself.[64]

Since the letters are an external matter, the light of the soul is enclothed within them in a very limited way and is absolutely hidden to the extent that (overtly) no life-energy can be appreciated, not even life-energy that resembles growth. Therefore, they are considered as inanimate matter.

From this perspective, the difference between the letters and all of the other powers of the soul is far greater than the differences among the other powers themselves. For all of the other powers affect and express the person's [character] itself; the light of the soul is revealed. (The difference between them is only in the degree and extent of that revelation, as will be explained.) With regard to letters, by contrast, their function is only to express and to reveal [the powers of the soul]. Therefore they resemble an entity that is distant from the soul.

(This parallels the relationship between inanimate matter and the other three forms of existence in the macrocosm. The fact that no life-energy at all is revealed in inanimate matter sets it aside from the other forms of existence to a far greater extent than the distinctions among the

---

63. [Trans. Note: By letters, the *sichah* refers to the potential for conscious thought and speech. These means of expression are considered as a power of the soul, for if they did not exist within the soul, the soul would be unable to use them. Nevertheless, they are external dimensions of an individual's personality. For the fact that a person is a capable speaker does not tell us anything about who he is. He may be able to speak about love, without having the tendency to manifest that emotion.]

64. Therefore they are called garments. [For although a person's garments may be representative of his character, they are, nevertheless, separate and distinct entities.] (See the explanation of this concept in the notes of the Rebbe Rashab to the *maamar* entitled *Posach Eliyahu* in *Torah Or*, and the *maamar* entitled *VihaEven HaZos*, 5673.)

other forms of existence in which the life-energy of the soul is revealed.)

IX. The parallel within man to the second type of existence, plant life, is the emotions. The emotions affect the soul and cannot at all be compared to stone, inanimate matter,[65] as the letters can. On the contrary, the emotions involve a tremendous amount of energy and activity. Nevertheless, the life-energy invested in the emotions is not comparable, and indeed, remarkably different from the life-energy that characterizes the intellect.

The very fact that the nature of emotions involves activity indicates that the emotions relate to a person as he is drawn out of his own sphere.[66] Intellect, by contrast, does not take a person out of his sphere. No matter how many concepts a person understands, he may remain calm. This shows that the emotions do not affect a person as he exists for himself. They affect only the dimension of soul that shares a connection with others.

[To explain: What motivates emotion?] The positive qualities — or the qualities that are not positive — of another person or entity affect a person and cause him to draw closer to that person or entity with feelings of love, or retreat with feelings of fear.

Since the emotions involve only the aspect of soul which has a connection to an outside entity — in contrast to intellect which involves the soul as it is for itself — the emotions are considered as closer to the quality of letters

---

65. [Trans. Note: Indeed, a "heart of stone" is a frequently used analogy to a person who does not express the positive emotional attributes which he possesses.]

66. [Trans. Note: The intent here is not that emotions involve communication with another being. On the contrary, emotions are largely self-contained (see sec. VII in the *sichah* from *Parshas Shmos* in this series). Instead, the intent is that emotions — like letters — reflect the aspect of a person's soul which functions in relation to the environment in which he lives. The soul — the person's influence as it exists for itself — is revealed in a diminutive manner.]

than to the intellect. For both letters and emotions are not connected to the soul as it is for itself. Both have a connection to other entities. (The difference is that the letters reflect only the influence drawn down from the soul, while the emotions affect the soul itself, as the soul is drawn outward.)

This resembles the relationship between the plant kingdom and the other three forms of existence in the macrocosm. For the life-energy of plants is bodily oriented. Therefore it is linked together with inanimate matter in the category of body, instead of being joined with animals and humans in the category of soul.

Just as the difference between animal and plant life is reflected in the fact that a plant is always rooted in a specific place, while an animal can move wherever it desires (as explained in section IV), so, too, we find a similar parallel with regard to emotion and intellect (the analogues to plants and animals in the microcosm [of our souls]).

Emotions (and even the intellect which relates to the emotions) as they exist in their own right are anchored in a specific tendency from which they cannot depart. As his character [is defined by] the nature of his emotions, a person whose nature reflects the attribute of *chesed* ([which is expressed in] love) must remain within that fundamental thrust. Within that thrust itself, there will be growth from an underdeveloped state to maturity. From underdeveloped states of love, he can precede to more advanced levels. [But his fundamental character remains the same.] A similar motif also applies to a person whose character thrust expresses *gevurah* (severity and might).

This is not true with regard to intellect. Firstly, intellect itself is not limited to a specific character thrust (for we see that a person can comprehend a concept which he cannot — due to the nature of his intellectual [not only his emotional] tendencies — tolerate). Moreover, because of the true and fundamental nature of intellect (i.e., the level of intellect that is above connection to the emotions), a person is capable of bringing about change within the character and nature of his emotions.[67]

Furthermore, within the realm of intellect itself, [despite the fact that each of the three qualities] *Chochmah, Binah,* and *Daas,* [have different fundamental thrusts,] there are several individuals [who manifest excellence in] all three areas. In the realm of emotions, by contrast, the attributes of *chesed* and *gevurah* cannot [coexist and work in harmony] unless the person modulates his emotions with intellect.[68]

X. Despite the above, the quality of intellect represents merely the analogue to the level of the animal within a person's soul. The human dimension (which is entirely distinct from the animal) is expressed in (the source for) the power of speech. Therefore, the term [in *Lashon HaKodesh*] used to describe humans is *midaber* (speaker) and not *maskil* (thinker).[69]

To explain: The spirituality and *peshitus* which rests within a person's intellect empowers him to go beyond his limits and choose any path he desires, even one which runs contrary to his nature (indeed, even one which requires him to change his nature). Nevertheless, this *peshitus* is still associated with defined existence. The reason a person chooses (based on his intellect) an approach that runs contrary to his emotional makeup is that his intellect — [which is also a] defined entity — requires him to do so.

---

67. See *Derech Mitzvosecha,* p. 84a; *Or HaTorah, Mishpatim,* p. 1134 (which explains that [intellect] reflects the level of *Beriah*).

68. See the *Sifri* which comments on the verse (*Devarim* 6:5): "There is no love in the place of fear, or fear in the place of love, except among the attributes of the Holy One, blessed be He."

69. See *Sefer HaMaamarim 5628,* p. 167, the series of *maamarim* entitled *VeKachah 5637,* ch. 22; *Toras Shalom,* p. 245.

    Sometimes it is explained that the reason a person is called a *midaber* is that speech is the first phase of the advantage that humans possess (the *maamar* entitled *BaChodesh HaShelishi,* 5702, ch. 4).

{Similar concepts apply with regard to the second dimension which expresses the spirituality humans possess (due to intellect) — the fact that "the spirit of man ascends upward." Although a person's quest to rise above himself takes him beyond his personal limits, nevertheless, [this too has an end-point]. For [this quest] stems from the fact that his intellect appreciates the advantage that exists in the higher level; (i.e., his mind forces him to understand that he is limited and there are matters that are above his intellect). Thus this [quests] itself stems from [and thus is bounded by] his personal existence.[70]

The power of speech, by contrast, reflects how a person is not bound by his own identity and can communicate with another individual. This unbounded quality is not connected with the person's own existence (for the potential to speak to another person does not stem from the fact that his own identity obligates him to speak to the other person, but from the fact that the source for this power comes from a very lofty place within the soul, a level where there are no definitions; there are no distinctions that separate one person from another). Thus the power of speech reflects the true concept of spirituality and *peshitus* possessed by the soul.[71]

---

70. [Trans. Note: Intellect will motivate only a limited measure of personal growth, for its own horizons are restricted — as a whole and for each person individually.]

71. [Trans. Note: Every entity in the spiritual cosmos is bound by its own specific identity. In our physical world, there are spatial distinctions that differentiate one entity from another. In the spiritual realms, the distinctions are not spatial, but reflect the nature of the entity. Each entity is what it is, and only what it is.

Every entity, whether spiritual or physical, cannot go beyond its identity. It is confined within its own set. Communication — sharing thoughts and feelings of substance — is a uniquely human potential. It stems from the fact that man is in essence more than himself, that his core is an unlimited spiritual entity. And moreover, that spiritual potential is not an abstract quality that remains hidden within the person's core, it affects his day-to-day existence. For man is a *midaber*, a speaker, sharing with others, showing self-transcendence as an ordinary part of his personal experience.]

XI. The explanation of the nature and type of distinctions among the four forms of existence: inanimate matter, plants, animals, and humans (in the world at large, and in the microcosm of every individual) gives us some understanding of the four spiritual realms: *Asiyah, Yetzirah, Beriah,* and *Atzilus.*

The initial[72] origins of personal existence (*yesh*) is the world of *Beriah.* Nevertheless, since in the world of *Beriah,* the *ayin* (the simplicity of G-dliness which transcends definition) shines [powerfully], the perception is that true existence is not *yesh* (the individual existence of the created beings), but the *ayin* which brings it into being. This feeling nullifies the sense of *yesh.* {This parallels animal life in which the body is subservient to the soul; indeed, the *mahus* (identity) of the body is the soul (as explained in section III). Or to cite another parallel: intellect (the animal in man) has the tendency to be attracted to what is above itself [even though] this involves losing its individual identity.[73]}

Therefore the *yesh* of the world of *Beriah* is described as "simple substance" without form [or definition],[74] in contrast to the *yesh* of the worlds of *Yetzirah* and *Asiyah* where the substance is already given form: in *Yetzirah,* a general form, and in *Asiyah,* a particular form. {This parallels the plant kingdom and inanimate matter in which the body is given precedence. For even in the plant kingdom, the body of the plant is not subservient to its life-energy. Or to cite

---

72. See the explanation of these concepts in the *maamar* entitled *Tzaaku,* 5688, *et al.*
73. See the letter of the Previous Rebbe (*HaTomim,* Vol. V, p. 61 (243), in which he quotes his father, the Rebbe Rashab) with regard to the *niggun* of four stanzas composed by the Alter Rebbe, explaining that the third stanza [which parallels the world of *Beriah*] shares a connection to the fourth stanza, and not to the second stanza, because "the world of *Beriah* is more closely connected to the world of *Atzilus* than to the world of *Yetzirah.* And {*Ibid.,* p. 63 (244)}: "The result of the third stanza is [a feeling of self-] *negation and transcendence.*"
74. [Trans. Note: I.e., the influence of *Atzilus* causes it to go beyond its distinctions.]

another parallel: the letters and the emotions which are both predominantly given over to entities outside oneself.}

Nevertheless, even the simple substance of the world of *Beriah* is still *yesh*, a substance and an entity. Its *peshitus* is only within the context of *yesh* (like intellect, which can be described as *peshitus*, but a *peshitus* that exists within the realm of definition, as explained in section X.)

The world of *Atzilus*, by contrast, is actual G-dliness.[75] It is entirely above the concept of *yesh*; it is *ayin*.[76]

XII. Although the four worlds of *Atzilus, Beriah, Yetzirah,* and *Asiyah* ([i.e.,] the spiritual dimension of the world of *Asiyah*) are spiritual realms, they, nevertheless, share certain points of commonality with the four forms of existence in our material world: inanimate matter, plants, animals, and humans (and the parallels that exist within our souls). Similarly, there is also a parallel to these levels in the root and source which brings into being (— and therefore is much higher —) than these four worlds, the four letters of G-d's name י-ה-ו-ה. ([Although it must be emphasized that these four letters represent spiritual levels] which are incomparably higher [than these material entities]), nevertheless, there is a similarity between these letters and the four forms of existence: inanimate matter, plants, animals, and humans which are drawn down from them after a vast process of descent and contraction.

---

75. *Tanya*, the beginning of *Tanya*, ch. 49.
76. [Trans. Note: The intent is that there is no sense of self in that realm and that the distinctions between the different attributes of G-dliness in the world of *Atzilus* allow for a perfect interrelation and fusion among themselves.

This clarification is necessary, for in some sources in *Chassidus*, it is explained that the origin of *yesh* is in the world of *Atzilus*. For in contrast to the levels above *Atzilus*, every attribute within *Atzilus* has already taken on its identity: *Chochmah* is *Chochmah*, and *chesed* is *chesed*. And yet, even as the attributes function within their own identities, there is a perfect sense of interrelation between them which stems from the fact that they are G-dliness and not *yesh*.]

Accordingly, we can appreciate that these four letters (including even the *yud*) do not represent the true *peshitus* of the *Or Ein Sof*. For these levels all share a connection to limited existence.

On this basis, we can appreciate the uniqueness of the fact that the Torah was given in connection with five קולות, i.e., it contains a fifth dimension which transcends all the four levels [mentioned above]. This represents true *peshitus*. This exemplifies the essence of the Torah, the level which is united with the essence of *Or Ein Sof*.

On this basis, we can appreciate why the connection between a bridegroom and the Torah is expressed in the fact that they both relate to five קולות. For the potential to conceive new life possessed by a bridegroom, (for "being fruitful and multiplying" is the purpose of a marriage,[77]) expresses the power of *Ein Sof*[78] which transcends all of the characteristics of the four forms of existence mentioned above.

XIII. Without minimizing the greatness of the essence G-dliness and the *peshitus* invested in the Torah which transcends the four letters of the name *Havayah*, [our Sages do not say that the Torah was given [only] with the fifth קול. Instead,] they emphasize that the Torah was given with five קולות. For when the Torah was given, the four levels which are connected to the four letters of G-d's name were also given. Indeed, the fifth and highest level was given together

---

77. For this reason, the explanation is given that the blessing *Shehechiyanu* is not recited together with the wedding blessings (*Gilayon Maharsha, Shulchan Aruch (Yoreh De'ah*, ch. 28, *Sifsei Kohen* subsection 5). [For until children are conceived, the purpose of a wedding is not consummated.] See *Likkutei Sichos*, Vol. V, pp. 118-119 and notes.
78. *Likkutei Torah, Shir HaShirim*, p. 40a.
   [Trans. Note: See also the *maamar* entitled *Sameach Tisamach 5657*, which explains at length that the conception of a child is one of the closest parallels to creation *yesh me'ayin*, something from nothing. Such creation is possible only through G-d's essential power (see *Tanya, Iggeres HaKodesh*, Epistle 20). And He granted man this power in order to bring children into the world.]

with them. For the Torah as a whole was given with five
קולות.

The reason for this is that [studying] the four levels of
the Torah awakens the four levels of the soul: *nefesh, ruach,*
neshamah, and *chayah.* And the fifth level arouses [the
essence of the soul,] the level of *yechidah* which is connected
with *yachid,* G-d's singular oneness.

All of the four levels of the Torah were given together[79]
so that the level of *yechidah* would [permeate and] shine
within the levels of *nefesh, ruach, neshamah,* and *chayah,*
which constitute a person's individual existence. For this
empowers him to make the world (which is composed of
four forms of existence: inanimate matter, plants, animals,
and humans) a dwelling for G-d's essence.[80]

(Adapted from *Sichos Shabbos Parshas Metzora,* 5717)

---

79. It is possible to explain that [the reason all five levels are revealed together]
is that when the level of *yechidah* (and the level of *yachid*) is revealed, everything is revealed. See the *maamar* entitled *Lehavin Inyan... HaNekudim* cited in
note 57.

80. [Trans. Note: The world is made a dwelling for G-d's essence through the
revelation of the fifth level. Nevertheless, if the fifth level was not given
together with the other four, that dwelling could not be "in the lower
worlds"; it could not permeate our material framework of reference. Instead,
its revelation would nullify the existence of our world. Through giving the
Torah with five קולות, G-d blended the fifth level together with the other four,
enabling His essence to be revealed within the context of limited existence.]

Parshas Pekudei

Likkutei Sichos, Vol. XVI, p. 475ff.

I. After the Torah describes the erection of the Sanctuary in detail,[1] it relates that the Divine Presence rested upon the Sanctuary, as it is written:[2] "And the cloud covered the Tent of Meeting and the glory of G-d filled the Sanctuary." That revelation was so powerful that "Moshe could not enter the Tent of Meeting, because the cloud rested upon it and the glory of G-d filled the Sanctuary."[3] The Torah then continues:[4] "When the cloud ascended from the Sanctuary, the children of Israel would journey forth on all their travels. And if the cloud did not ascend, they would not journey forth until it did ascend."

These verses present a difficulty: On the surface, the concluding verses which speak about the journeys of the Jewish people in the desert belong — where they are indeed repeated (and elaborated upon) — in *Parshas Behaalos'cha.*[5] What is the connection between the pattern of the Jews' journeys (— that "when the cloud... [they] would journey forth.... And if the cloud did not ascend, they would not journey forth..." —) with the content of our Torah reading which speaks of the Divine Presence resting in the Sanctuary?

---

1. *Shmos* 40:17ff.
2. *Ibid.*:34.
3. *Ibid.*:35.
4. *Ibid.*:36-37.
5. See *Bamidbar* 9:15ff.

The *Seforno*[6] [attempts to resolve this question], explaining that the fact that the Jews would journey forth when the cloud ascended demonstrated the permanence with which the Divine Presence rested within the Sanctuary. "For it would not withdraw at all until the Jewish people had to journey forth."

On the surface, however, this explanation does not resolve the issue. For the wording of the verse appears to indicate that its intent is to relate the pattern of the Jewish people's journeys. As the *Midrash*[7] states: "This is the description of the journeys." And thus, the question remains: What is the connection between the "description of the journeys" which are detailed at length in *Parshas Behaalos'cha* with the story of the erection of the Sanctuary and the manifestation of G-d's Presence within it?

This question is reinforced by our Sages' statements[8] that note the connection between the beginning of *Parshas Vayikra,*[9] "And He called to Moshe," and its preceding verse ("When the cloud ascended...) Moshe could not enter the Tent of Meeting." [Our Sages explain: because "Moshe could not enter,"] G-d "called to Moshe" and made it possible for him to go into the Tent of Meeting.

Thus it appears that between the verses that follow in sequence — "Moshe could not enter..." and "And He called to Moshe" — the Torah interrupts the conceptual flow and mentions a peripheral matter — the description of the journeys which is seemingly unrelated to the Sanctuary.

II. All concepts in the Torah are precise. Since the *Midrash* explains that "And He called to Moshe" (the beginning of the Book of *Vayikra*) comes in sequence to the conclusion of

---

6.   In his commentary to the conclusion of this *parshah*.
7.   The *Lekach Tov* in its commentary to this verse.
8.   *Midrash Tanchuma*, the beginning of *Parshas Vayikra*, sec. 1, 8; *Zohar*, Vol. III, p. 3b; *Lekach Tov, loc. cit.; Midrash Tanchuma, Parshas Behaalos'cha*, sec. 6, *et al.*
9.   *Vayikra* 1:1.

Parshas Pekudei, "Moshe could not enter," there is a thematic connection shared by the Torah readings in which these verses are included.

The Book of *Vayikra,* the Book of the Sacrifices,[10] follows not only the narrative of the construction and the erection of the Sanctuary (the place where the sacrifices are offered), but also the particular description of the manner in which G-d's Presence rested in the Sanctuary. This is the theme of *Parshas Pekudei,* and particularly, of the concluding passages.

It is possible to explain that this is the reason why after the Torah states: "And Moshe could not enter...," it makes an interruption and mentions the journeys of the Jewish people which are associated with "the cloud ascend[ing] from the Sanctuary," i.e., the withdrawal of G-d's Presence. The spiritual import of the sacrifices is associated with the concept that for the Jews to journey forth [from their encampments] G-d's Presence had to ascend from the Sanctuary. (As will be explained in section VIII,) [this factor is] more [significant] than the actual indwelling of G-d's Presence in that structure.

III. The above matters can be resolved by prefacing [another concept]: the connection between the conclusion of the Book of *Shmos* with its beginning (following the principle:[11] "The end is rooted in the beginning, and the beginning in the end"). This is reflected by the fact that the names of both the first and the last *parshiyos* of the book are related to the concept of counting.

[The name of the first *parshah,*] *Shmos,* [is related to counting,] as *Rashi* states: "Although [the Torah] counted them [previously]... it counts them again... to show their dearness, that they are compared to stars." And *Pekudei,* [which means "reckoning," certainly relates to that concept,

---

10. See the commentary of the *Ramban* in his introduction to *Sefer Vayikra.*
11. *Sefer Yetzirah* 1:7.

for it includes] the account "of the *shekalim* donated to the Sanctuary... all its utensils, for its service."[12]

Now the theme of the Book of *Shmos* is the redemption of the Jewish people[13] from Egypt. It thus appears that the theme of redemption is connected with the concept of counting (which connects the beginning[14] and the conclusion[15] of the text). A conceptual difficulty thus arises, for seemingly counting and redemption are two opposite concepts. "The very fact that an entity can be counted" — indicates that the entity is limited (and thus can be reckoned in a tally). Counting thus emphasizes the theme of limitation. Redemption (in its ultimate sense), by contrast, reflects the departure from Egypt, i.e., the transcendence of exile and limitation.[16]

This fusion of opposites is reflected in the beginning of the book itself. The name of the Torah reading (which reflects the theme of the entire Torah reading) is *Shmos*, which refers to the limitations[17] implied by the counting of "the children of Israel who came into Egypt." And directly afterwards, the verse relates:[18] "And the children of Israel were fruitful, increased, multiplied, and became very, very powerful," indicating a population explosion far beyond the ordinary norm. This verse is also part of the *parshah* of

---

12. *Rashi*, the beginning of *Parshas Pekudei*. See similar concepts in the commentaries of the *Rashbam*, the *Ramban*, and others.
13. Thus the *Ramban* (at the conclusion of *Parshas Pekudei*) refers to the book as *Sefer HaGeulah*, "the Book of Redemption." Similarly, *Bereishis Rabbah* 3:5 [refers to *Shmos* as the book which chronicles how] "Israel went out from darkness to light." See also *Shmos Rabbah* 1:5 which states that the names of the tribes mentioned in the beginning of the book are mentioned in association with "the redemption of Israel."
14. And the beginning and "head" of every entity includes the entire content of that entity.
15. And "everything follows the conclusion" (*Berachos* 12a).
16. Note also *Torah Or* (p. 71c ff.) which states that the exodus from Egypt reflects the transcendence of all the boundaries and limitations within the spiritual cosmos.
17. I.e., it refers to no more than 70 souls as stated in verse 5.
18. *Shmos* 1:7.

Shmos. Thus this prodigious growth is also a part of the "counting" of the Jewish people.

Similarly, the conclusion of the book *[Parshas Pekudei]*, which recounts the reckoning of [the donations for [the Sanctuary], also obviously reflects limitation (for all the vessels of the Sanctuary were of a limited number and size). Nevertheless, the conclusion of the *parshah:* "Moshe could not enter the Tent of Meeting, because the cloud rested upon it and the glory of G-d filled the Sanctuary," reflects the unlimited manifestation of the Divine Presence in the Tent of Meeting. [Its transcendence was so great that] even Moshe, "the most select of all men,"[19] [could not approach it].

IV. In general, the concept can be explained as follows: The ultimate goal is that we should transcend limitations and reach the redemption, a level beyond the measures and limitations of our world. The intent is not, however, that the transcendence will nullify the existence of this limited framework, but that there will be a fusion of infinity and finiteness.[20]

---

19. *Rambam,* the Commentary to the *Mishnah* (Sanhedrin, Introduction to ch. 10, the Seventh Principle).

20. For it is such a fusion that reveals G-d's essence, a level that transcends all limitations entirely, with nothing being beyond its potential. It has the capacity to join limitation and transcendence together (see *Likkutei Sichos,* Vol. III, p. 904ff.).

   For this reason, the names of the *parshiyos* (Pekudei and Shmos) express the concept of counting. For it is through the concept of limitation that G-d's essence can be tapped (see the explanation of this concept in *Likkutei Sichos, loc. cit.,* p. 905, which explains that for this reason, the Divine service of prayer must be associated with a specific place).

   [Trans. Note: The intent is that finiteness itself cannot represent G-d's essence, for He is utterly unlimited and cannot be circumscribed within any limited scope. And yet, our ordinary conception of infinity is also not appropriate for G-d's essence. For we generally conceive of infinity as the opposite of finiteness, a transcendent and boundless quality. Associating infinity with transcendence alone also indicates that it is not G-d's essence. For infinity — like finiteness — has a specific scope; it is infinite and not finite. He, by

{We see this concept expressed with regard to the counting of the Jewish people, as it is written:[21] "And the number of the children of Israel will be as the sands of the sea which cannot be measured and cannot be counted," i.e., there will be a number, and that number will "not be measured, nor counted."

A similar concept applies with regard to the Sanctuary. [G-d's Presence,] which is unlimited and unbounded, came to rest in (the vessels of) the Sanctuary which are measured and limited entities.}

[The rationale for this is] that G-d's intent is [defined by our Sages as follows:] "The Holy One, blessed be He, desired a dwelling in the lower realms."[22] This implies two dimensions:

a) There must be a dwelling for G-d's essence[23] (which transcends our worldly frame of reference entirely); and

b) That dwelling shall be in "the lower worlds,"[24] i.e., in this material world, below which there is none, (i.e., a limited and bounded framework).

V. These two dimensions — that the dwelling be for G-d's essence, and that it be in the lower realms — reflect the difference between the Jewish people and the world at large.

The (inner) dimension of G-d's dwelling is "to dwell and rest within the souls of the Jewish people... that they become a resting place in which He dwells."[25] Since "the

contrast, is absolutely unbounded. Neither infinity, nor finiteness describes Him, and neither can be disassociated from Him.]

21. *Hoshea* 2:1. See the *maamar* of that title and its explanation in *Likkutei Torah, Bamidbar*, p. 6a ff., 7c ff., *et al.* See also the extensive explanation in *Likkutei Sichos*, Vol. XIX, pp. 24, 26ff.
22. *Tanya*, ch. 36, based on *Midrash Tanchuma, Parshas Naso*, sec. 16.
23. *Or HaTorah, Parshas Balak*, p. 997; the series of *maamarim* entitled *Yom Tov Shel Rosh HaShanah*, 5666, p. 3, *et al.*
24. *Tanya, loc. cit.*
25. The series of *maamarim* entitled *Yom Tov Shel Rosh HaShanah*, 5666, p. 468. See also *Torah Or, Parshas Mishpatim*, p. 764; *Or HaTorah*, p. 1267; *Sefer HaMamaarim 5630*, p. 64; *Sefer HaMamaarim 5670*, p. 199ff.

Holy One, blessed be He, and Israel are one,"²⁶ the Jewish
people are the true dwelling for G-d's essence, for they are
one with His essence.²⁷

{The concept of "a dwelling in the lower realms" for the
world at large,²⁸ by contrast, is (merely) that the world will
appreciate that the totality of its existence stems from G-d's
essence; "aside from Him, there is absolutely no existence
at all."²⁹}

This dwelling is established in the lower worlds,
through the Divine service of the Jewish people in this
material realm, by making physical entities a medium for
G-dliness. For it is through these efforts that the source of
the Jewish souls — the level at which they are united with
G-d's essence — is revealed.³⁰

To use slightly different wording: When will it be
revealed that the Jews are a dwelling for G-d — that they
are united with G-d's essence in a consummate manner,
without any limitations and restraints? When the limits and
bounds of this material world do not present any constraint,

---

26. See *Zohar*, Vol. III, p. 73a, and 93b. See also our Sages' (*Shir HaShirim Rabbah* 5:3) interpretation of the term "My perfect one" (*Shir HaShirim* 5:2), as "My twin." See also *Likkutei Torah, Shir HaShirim*, pp. 34d, 39a.

27. See *Likkutei Sichos*, Vol. V, p. 246 (translated in this series), which explains that [because the Jews are one with G-d, as it were] they can experience "the satisfaction of the Creator" which incomparably surpasses the realm of the created beings.

   [Trans. Note: Only an entity which is entirely one with G-d can become a dwelling for Him. Because the Jewish people do not have an identity apart from G-dliness, they can become a dwelling for Him. The world at large, by contrast, has a definition of its own and exists as an apparently separate entity. As such, it cannot be united with Him in a complete manner.]

28. See *Likkutei Sichos, loc. cit.*, and Vol. VI, p. 236 (and note 13) [also translated in this series]. For this reason, the world is merely a medium through which G-d's intent for the creation can be fulfilled, but the intent is not within it itself.

29. See the *maamar* entitled *ViLekachtem*, 5661. See also *Likkutei Sichos*, Vol. XII, p. 75, the marginal notes to note 30.

30. See the series of *maamarim* entitled *Yom Tov Shel Rosh HaShanah*, 5666, p. 492ff., *et al.* See *Likkutei Sichos, loc. cit.*, p. 74ff.

and instead, the lower realms themselves become a fit place for His dwelling.[31]

VI. Based on the above, we can appreciate why the beginning of the Book of *Shmos* speaks about the counting of the Jewish people, and the conclusion of the book speaks about the reckoning of the vessels of the Sanctuary.

The Book of *Bereishis* speaks about the creation itself,[32] how it existed before focus was placed on its intent:[33] [that it was created] "for the sake of the Jewish people and for the sake of the Torah."[34] The Book of *Shmos,* in contrast, speaks about the children of Israel, (how they were conceived[35] [as a people] and how they became the Jewish

31. Therefore the fact that G-d's dwelling is established in the lower worlds is not an ancillary element of its existence. For since the intent for a dwelling in the lower realms stems from G-d's essence, it is impossible to say that it is a composite of two factors (see *Likkutei Sichos,* Vol. V, p. 245, note 36). Instead, this dimension is pertinent to the establishment of the dwelling itself.

[Trans. Note: To summarize this section of the *sichah:* Since the definition of a dwelling is a place where G-d's essence is revealed, it follows that this dwelling can only be within the souls of the Jewish people. For they alone are utterly one with G-d, while existence at large has a separate identity and thus cannot be an appropriate vessel for the manifestation of G-d's presence.

On the other hand, for G-d's essence — and not merely His revealed powers — to be manifest within the Jewish people, they must descend and carry out their Divine service within this material world. For in the higher spiritual levels of existence, the emphasis is on revealed dimensions of G-dliness. In this material world, in contrast, the challenges this spiritual environment present require a Jew to tap the essential spark of G-d within his soul. When he succeeds in this challenge, he expresses how our world is a dwelling for G-d. Similarly, on a more cosmic scale, when the Jews as a whole complete their Divine service within the world, it will be evident that every element of existence is part of His dwelling.]

32. As the *Midrash* (*Bereishis Rabbah* 3:5) states: "In its [narrative, it is told] how the Holy One, blessed be He, became involved and created His world."

33. Nevertheless, this is also a portion of the Torah. For in order for the Divine intent in the establishment of a dwelling in the lower realms to be consummated, it is necessary that at the outset, the intent of the creation be concealed within it [— this is the definition of the term "lower realms" —] and that the Jews — through their Divine service — make the world into a dwelling for Him.

34. *Osios d'Rabbi Akiva* 2; Rashi, *Bereishis* 1:1 et al.

35. See *Yechezkel,* ch. 16, and commentaries.

nation), and the Torah. [These are the mediums] through which the intent of the creation are expressed. In this [endeavor], (i.e., the Jews' efforts to carry out the purpose of the creation,) there is a beginning and a conclusion.

The beginning (the essence and the inner dimension) of the intent is the Jewish people as they are connected with G-d's essence. This is reflected in the counting of the Jewish people recounted in *Parshas Shmos* which "makes known the dearness of the Jewish people." (Therefore, it is G-d Himself who counts the people — and He counts them in the Torah.)

The conclusion — i.e., how the intent is actually expressed — is through making a Sanctuary for G-d from material entities.[36]

VII. The source of the souls of the Jewish people (as they are one with G-d's essence) is revealed through their Divine service in the lower realms — in a place of concealment and hiddenness. Accordingly, it can be understood that this is accomplished {to an even greater extent than through building the Sanctuary — for this was a place where G-dliness was revealed[37]} through Divine service that involves an entity of the lower realms which is not — as it defines itself — a medium for G-dliness. In a more general sense, this refers to our Divine service in the era of exile when G-dliness is not apparent in the world.

---

36. To use slightly different wording: There are two dimensions to G-d's dwelling in the lower realms:

a) the inner dimension of the dwelling; this is achieved within the Jewish people, for their existence is [an expression of] G-d's essence;

b) the external dimension of the world, i.e., that the world becomes a place which is fit for the essence to be revealed. {Nevertheless, as explained in note 31, this intent is not, Heaven forbid, a composite of two thrusts.}

37. [Trans. Note: Although building the Sanctuary involved material entities, since G-d's Presence was revealed within it, it did not express entirely the theme of "a dwelling in the lower worlds." That theme is most consummately expressed when Divine service is carried out in a place where G-dliness is not openly apparent.]

This is the reason why, at the conclusion of the account of the work involved in constructing the Sanctuary and the manifestation of the Divine Presence within, [the Torah] tells about the journeys of the Jewish people which are associated with "the ascent of the cloud." For the ultimate intent of the Sanctuary (which involves making the lower realms a dwelling for G-d) is achieved primarily through (the potential granted by the Sanctuary[38]) to carry out "all your journeys."

In this vein, the Alter Rebbe explains[39] that the journeys of the Jewish people through the desert (also) allude to the refinement of the "wilderness of the nations"[40] [through the Divine service carried out] throughout the era of exile. In this era, the Divine Presence is also in exile; it is not revealed. {[This is alluded to by] the ascent of the cloud [which indicates] the withdrawal of the Divine Presence.} [Nevertheless,] the Jews refine and transform the concealment of the world, causing G-dliness to shine within.

VIII. The above concept (— that the ultimate goal of the Sanctuary is achieved through the Divine service performed outside the Sanctuary —) is expressed within the Sanctuary itself, in the fact that the primary service performed in the Sanctuary was sacrificial worship.[41]

---

38. [Trans. Note: The Rebbe emphasizes that the Divine service with lower, worldly entities is dependent on the influence of the Sanctuary, i.e., a place where G-dliness is openly revealed. For the desired Divine service involves not merely establishing a connection with the lower realms, but making them into a dwelling, a place where G-dliness is evident.}

39. The *maamarim* entitled *Eileh Maasei* in *Likkutei Torah*; see also the sources quoted in the following note.

40. Cf. *Yechezkel* 20:35. See the commentaries of Rabbeinu Bacheya, the *Or HaChayim*, and others to the beginning of *Parshas Maasei*; see also *Likkutei Torah*, the beginning of *Parshas Nasso, et al.*

41. Note the *Rambam's* [definition of the *mitzvah* to build a Sanctuary in the *Mishneh Torah*], *Hilchos Beis HaBechirah*, "to build a house for G-d, prepared for sacrifices to be offered within." (See also similar statements in *Sefer HaMitzvos*, pos. commandment 20, and general principle 12.)

The difference between the Sanctuary and the offering of the sacrifices can be explained as follows: With regard to the construction of the Sanctuary, the ultimate purpose was {primarily not to elevate the material entities from which the Sanctuary was constructed, but} to create a place in this material realm where the Divine Presence could rest from above. (The manifestation of G-d's Presence is incomparably above [the entire realm of] material entities.) The intent of offering the sacrifices,[42] by contrast, was to refine and elevate the physical animal [being offered] and transform it into a sacrifice for G-d, making it a sacred object.

The sacrificial worship (and the drawing down of holiness it brings about) is a preparation to reach a higher level, the manifestation [of G-d's Presence] in the Sanctuary, (and more particularly, in the ark).

{This is reflected in the diminutive form of the *alef* in the word *Vayikra* [which begins the following book of the Torah], for it alludes to *tzimtzum*, contraction.[43] For sacrificial worship (the theme of the Book of *Vayikra*) relates to the light of holiness as it is drawn down (— *vayikra* [means "and He called," i.e.,] referring to [G-dly light] as it is called forth and drawn down[44] —) which is a lesser level than the manifestation of G-d's Presence in the Sanctuary.[45]}

See also *Likkutei Sichos*, Vol. IV, p. 1346, note 24 [which explains] the *Ramban's* (commentary to the Torah, the beginning of *Parshas Terumah*) position that the manifestation of G-d's Presence in the Holy Ark is His primary desire for the Sanctuary. [This, however, is G-d's purpose for the existence of the Sanctuary. It does not necessarily] reflect His intent with regard to the *mitzvos* which the Jews were commanded to perform within the Sanctuary (man's Divine service). See also *Likkutei Sichos*, Vol. XVI, p. 438ff.

42. See the *maamar* entitled *Vihu Omaid*, 5663 [*Sefer HaMaamarim 5663*, p. 50ff.] (Kehot, 5713).

43. *Likkutei Torah, Vayikra*, p. 1b.

44. *Ibid.* (the beginning of sec. 2); see also *Tanya*, the conclusion of ch. 37.

45. See *Likkutei Torah, op. cit.*, (1b) which states: "A ray is drawn down for him that enables him *afterwards* to enter the Tent of Meeting."

Nevertheless, it is through this activity that it is possible to reach a higher intent in the Sanctuary,[46] to make the material entities themselves mediums for G-dliness.[47]

On this basis, we can appreciate how *Vayikra*, "And He called to Moshe," (and the entire Book of Sacrifices) follows in conceptual sequence to [the verse] "When the cloud ascended..." ([one of the questions raised] in section II), for they both underscore the same point — that the intent of the Sanctuary should be fulfilled. Indeed, that intent is fulfilled even more in a place where the Divine Presence is not manifest in the Sanctuary.

IX. The Divine service [of the Jewish people] during their journeys lacks the revelation of the Divine Presence. Nevertheless,[48] these efforts bring into revelation the source of the souls of the Jewish people, the point at which they are united with G-d's essence as explained above.

This is the inner intent of the verse: "When the cloud ascended from the Sanctuary, the children of Israel would journey forth on all their travels." On an apparent level, the Divine Presence did withdraw. From an inner perspective,

---

46. Nonetheless, since the sacrificial worship was also performed in the Sanctuary, the concept of establishing a dwelling in the lower realms was fulfilled in a more consummate manner through the journeys of the Jewish people through the desert. It is possible to explain that this is the reason why the details of the journeys of the Jewish people are elaborated upon only in the Book of *Bamidbar* (which follows the Book of *Vayikra*). *Bamidbar* ("in the desert") reflects the refinement of "the desert of nations."

47. [Trans. Note: See *Likkutei Sichos*, Vol. VI, p. 18ff (translated in this series) which explains the advantage of the *Beis HaMikdash* (where the material entities themselves became holy) over the Sanctuary (which reflected primarily the manifestation of G-dliness).]

48. This paralles [the pattern] described in the conclusion of [the section], *Chinuch Kattan*, in *Tanya*:

> One must proceed from level to level... Between one level and another, before one reaches the higher level, one is in a fallen state [when compared] to one's original level.

Perhaps this is the same concept described above. {See the first reason for this fall explained in the notes to *Chinuch Kattan* by R. Hillel of Paritch ([printed at] the conclusion of *Pelach HaRimon, Bereishis*).}

however, their Divine service [on their journeys] is rooted
in a level which is higher than the cloud [which manifested
G-d's Presence in] the Sanctuary. This level was drawn
down [and manifest] in their next encampment. [In that
vein, we can appreciate *Rashi's* commentary[49] which inter-
prets] "their journeys" as referring to the place of their
encampment.

This provides a lesson for every individual in his Divine
service. Despite the darkness of the exile, and despite the
inner exile in which each person appreciates that he is
found, he should know that [this journey will lead to a positive conclusion].

[A person must be committed to] carrying out the
Divine mission "in all their journeys" — i.e., regardless of
what the journey is, as long as it is associated with "the
cloud of G-d," [as it is written] "when the cloud ascended
from the Sanctuary, the children of Israel would journey
forth... and if the cloud did not ascend, they would not
journey forth" — for "From G-d, man's footstep are established."[50] Wherever a person goes, in every situation in
which he finds himself, he is given a mission from G-d to
establish a dwelling for Him in the lower realms. Therefore
his journey through exile is in accordance with G-d's will.

[With this approach,] he will appreciate a positive
dimension of "the cloud ascend[ing]"; he will reach a higher
level than the cloud. (Although the revelation of the cloud
surpasses even the potential of the spark of Moshe Rabbeinu which he possesses within his soul,[51] [he will be able to
reach an even higher level]). He will then draw down this
level in the encampment which follows until he reaches the
rung at which "Israel and the Holy One, blessed be He, are
all one."

(Adapted from *Sichos Shabbos Parshas Pekudei*, 5724, 5727)

---

49. *Shmos* 40:38.
50. *Tehillim* 37:23; see *HaYom Yom*, pp. 69, 104.
51. See *Tanya*, ch. 42.